WALKING

THE MOURNE MOUNTAINS

by
Andrew
McCluggage

About the Author

Andrew McCluggage is an outdoor writer and photographer from Northern Ireland. After 20 years as a corporate lawyer, he decided to do something interesting and started writing walking guidebooks.

His first book was Walking in the Briançonnais, covering a beautiful part of the French Alps. Since then, he has written a variety of guidebooks for hiking and trekking.

Other Knife Edge Outdoor Guidebooks written by Andrew include:

- **Tour du Mont Blanc**
- **Walker's Haute Route: Chamonix to Zermatt**
- **Tour of the Écrins National Park (GR54)**

The twin summits of Cock Mountain viewed from the summit of Hen Mountain

Publisher: Knife Edge Outdoor Limited (NI648568)
12 Torrent Business Centre, Donaghmore, County Tyrone, BT70 3BF, UK
www.knifeedgeoutdoor.com

First edition 2019

ISBN: 978-1-912933-03-7

A catalogue record for this book is available from the British Library

Front cover: Walking alongside the Mourne Wall towards Rocky Mountain
Introduction page: The incredible ridge travelled on Walks 10 and 11

Contents

Newcastle town centre

All routes described in this guide have been recently walked by the author and both the author and publisher have made all reasonable efforts to ensure that all information is as accurate as possible. However, while a printed book remains constant for the life of an edition, things in the countryside often change. Trails are subject to forces outside our control: for example, landslides, tree-falls or other matters can result in damage to paths or route changes; waymarks and signposts may fade or be destroyed by wind, snow or the passage of time; or trails may not be maintained by the relevant authorities. If you notice any discrepancies between the contents of this guide and the facts on the ground, then please let us know. Our contact details can be found at the back of this book.

Getting Help

Emergency Services Number: dial 999 and ask for Mountain Rescue.

Distress Signal

The signal that you are in distress is 6 blasts on a whistle spaced over a minute, followed by a minute's silence. Then repeat. The response that your signal has been received is 3 blasts of a whistle over a minute followed by a minute's silence. At night, flashes of a torch can also be used in the same sequences. **Always carry a torch and whistle.**

Signalling to a Helicopter from the Ground

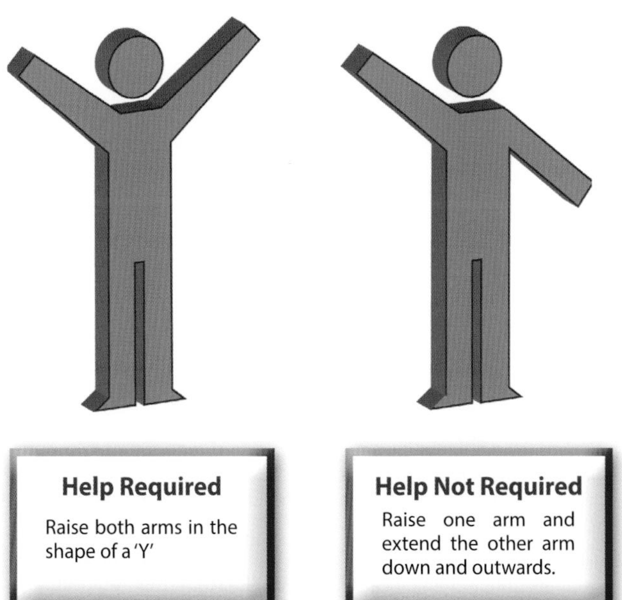

WARNING

Hills and mountains can be dangerous places and walking is a potentially dangerous activity. Many of the routes described in this guide cross exposed and potentially hazardous terrain. You walk entirely at your own risk. It is solely your responsibility to ensure that you and all members of your group have adequate experience, fitness and equipment. Neither the author nor the publisher accepts any responsibility or liability whatsoever for death, injury, loss, damage or inconvenience resulting from use of this book, participation in the activity of mountain walking or otherwise.

Note that all land in Northern Ireland is owned privately or by the Crown so there may be no legal right of entry to the land.

The path along the Slieve Binnian ridge

Introduction

Slieve Donard emerges from a sea of cloud

The Mourne range comprises the highest mountains in Northern Ireland. It is a stunning wilderness which is popular with local walkers but is relatively unknown to those outside of Ireland. The highest mountain in the range is Slieve Donard (849m), Northern Ireland's highest point, which sweeps majestically down into the Irish Sea at the pretty seaside town of Newcastle. This proximity to the sea is a characteristic of the Mournes, often creating a mysterious atmosphere, because frequently, the high peaks can be seen rising dramatically out of a blanket of sea mist. Summiting a Mourne peak by climbing out above the cloud line is an unforgettable experience.

The Mournes have everything you would expect from a mountain region on the Emerald Isle: beautifully long ridges, magnificent summits and vibrant heather and gorse covered slopes. However, there is one key thing which sets it apart: uniquely, the whale-backed slopes of the highest peaks are completely encircled by the lovely dry-stone 'Mourne Wall' ('MW') which was completed in 1922. The MW was designed to protect the water catchment area for the Silent Valley Reservoir and so it runs, with hardly a break, along the ridges, and up over the main peaks, of the range. The MW is painstakingly maintained in excellent condition and provides a stunning counterpoint to the magnificent scenery.

Like most of the mountains on the Island of Ireland, the range can be walked in all seasons and each season has its merits: spring with the bright yellow gorse flowers; summer with its long days, purple heather and blue skies; autumn with its golden light; while a snowy day alongside the MW in winter is very special indeed.

Those used to walking in more populated places such as England or the USA will, by comparison, find the Mournes to be quiet. Many walkers focus on Slieve Donard because it is the highest peak in the range. However, elsewhere it is not uncommon to spend a day in these wonderful mountains hardly encountering another soul.

Although Northern Ireland has a troubled past, it and the vast majority of its people have undergone significant change in the last two decades. Most significantly, there is peace and consequently, visitors have flooded in to see this magnificent little country. Fighting between terrorist organisations has been replaced by oral bickering between politicians. Terrorist activity in Northern Ireland is no more likely than in any other part of Europe. Belfast itself is now a popular city break destination. Those who let the past put them off will miss out on the warmth of the people, evocative scenery enjoyed in relative solitude, fabulous food and, of course, a properly poured Guinness. And make no mistake, an Irish stout bought and drunk on the Island of Ireland is worth three bought and drunk elsewhere. It is no myth that Guinness, unlike hikers, does not travel well!

The Mourne Wall (MW)

The MW is 35km long (22 miles), up to 2.4m high and about 1m wide (on average). It is an amazing feat of engineering, built with locally sourced granite, which runs almost unbroken along the ridges, and up over 15 of the peaks, of the Mournes. In fact, the only real gaps in this man-made structure are the few places where the wall meets cliffs and rocks and nature had already done the job itself.

Ask the Author

If you have any questions which are not answered by this book, then you can ask the author on our Facebook Group, 'Hiking in the Mourne Mountains'

So what is the story of this magnificent structure? Why was it painstakingly built, stone by stone, on the top of a bunch of mountains? Well it all had to do with water and a growing population. The problem of a reliable water supply for Belfast was first identified by the Corporation of Belfast in the 1670s. By the end of the 19th century, a growing urban population and the development of industries such as linen and ship building had greatly exacerbated the problem. The Belfast Water Commissioners identified the valley basins of the Mourne Mountains as a solution (given the high rainfall and lack of pollution). The Commissioners promptly purchased 9,000 acres of the Mournes and commenced an ambitious schedule of infrastructure works which took many decades.

The works eventually included diverting water from the Annalong and Kilkeel rivers to a reservoir close to Belfast; constructing a dam across the Silent Valley (1923 to 1933); digging a 3.6km tunnel through Slieve Binnian to transport water from the Annalong Valley to the Silent Valley (1949 to 1952); and building a second dam to create the Ben Crom reservoir (1954 to 1957). However, one of the earliest stages of the scheme was the construction of the MW (1904 to 1922). This was built to protect the water catchment area from interference, and pollution, by both humans and animals. The MW almost completely enclosed the Commissioners' 9,000 acre site.

The MW is still largely in pristine condition even though no mortar was used in its construction (except in the three stone shelters built on Slieve Donard, Slieve Commedagh and Slieve Meelmore). Its longevity is a testament to the hardy folk who braved all seasons to build it by hand, stone by stone.

The MW was not universally popular though. In his book 'Mourne Country' (originally published in 1951), E. Estyn Evans wrote:

> *'This giant wall, of dry-stone construction, strides over the mountains regardless of the contours, a monument to the skill of its builders. Its broad top offers a convenient short-cut to the summits, but one must regret that it was ever built. It breaks the skyline, obstructs the views and destroys the wild beauty of the High Mournes'*

Most modern walkers would disagree with the latter of these sentiments. Viewed in the 21st century, the MW is a beautiful structure in itself built using methods and craftsmanship that are largely extinct today. As a landmark among the mountains, it somehow seems to blend in appropriately and provides a stunning counterpoint to the magnificent scenery. A glance through the photographs in this book will demonstrate that the MW and the mountains appear to have a somewhat symbiotic relationship. The MW is now so pivotal to the atmosphere of the Mournes that without it they would lose some of the originality and character that make them so special.

On a more practical note, the presence of the MW is comforting and reassuring for the walker. On key sections of many walks, you can simply follow the MW which simplifies navigation and provides a 'security blanket' in times of low visibility. Accordingly, it is understandable that those who know the Mournes well view the MW with a mixture of respect, affection and admiration.

The much loved Mourne Wall

Tollymore Forest Park

Tollymore is a beautiful forest park of approximately 630 hectares situated in the foothills of the Mourne Mountains, right next to the range's highest peaks. It is much more interesting than the average forest due to the quirky follies which were tastefully sprinkled throughout the park. Gothic gate arches, magnificent 'Billy Goat Gruff' stone bridges, numerous pointy turrets, grottos and caves are all found here and make exploring the park a delight. The follies were influenced by Thomas Wright of Durham, a friend of James Hamilton, 1st Earl of Clanbrassil.

The early history of the park is confusing but, from what information is available, it would appear that, after the Norman invasion of Ulster in 1177 and the creation of the Earldom of Ulster, the balance of power in the area shifted to the Magennis clan which by the 15th century controlled much of the land in south County Down, including what is now Tollymore Forest Park. In 1611, Tollymore and other lands were surrendered to the English Crown in return for a formal freehold in the name of Brian McHugh McAghorley Magennis. In 1628, Tollymore passed to Brian Magennis' grandson who died childless in the 1660s. At this point Tollymore passed to Brian Magennis' only daughter Ellen, who was married to Captain William Hamilton.

On William Hamilton's death in 1674, the land was passed to his son James. James Hamilton died in 1701 and Tollymore was passed in turn to his son (William Hamilton's grandson), James, who became Viscount Limerick and 1st Earl of Clanbrassil (second creation).

The Hamilton family remained owners of Tollymore until 1798 when the great grandson of William Hamilton, also called James, died without an heir. Tollymore was then transferred to his sister Anne, who married Robert Jocelyn, Earl of Roden. The Roden family owned Tollymore until the estate was sold by Robert Jocelyn, 8th Earl of Roden to the Ministry of Agriculture between 1930 and 1941. In 1955 the forest was opened to the public and it was the first forest park on the Island of Ireland to encourage visitors.

During the 1800s, the forest contained five saw mills for processing felled trees. The mills were located on the banks of the Shimna River and powered by water. Millponds stored water which was released during dry periods to turn the water wheels. The millponds can still be located.

Haystacks near Carrick Little

The Mourne Way

From time to time, while walking in the Mournes, you may come across waymarks for the Mourne Way. This is a long distance route of approximately 40km which travels between Newcastle and Rostrevor along the northern fringes of the Mourne range. It is almost entirely off-road. The scenery is spectacular although it avoids climbing any of the high peaks. Some people walk the route in one long summer's day but we prefer to split it into two sections, with an overnight bivouac. Unfortunately, the waymarks are sporadic. Further information can be found at www.walkni.com.

Game of Thrones locations

Everybody knows that Northern Ireland served as a stunning backdrop for many of the finest scenes in Game of Thrones, the incredibly addictive television series. But working out exactly where the locations are can be quite tricky. As far as we can discern, the following three Mourne Mountain places were used as Game of Thrones locations:

- **Sandy Brae near Attical:** in season one, the countryside here was used as the entrance to Vaes Dothrak. Walks 21 and 22 use Sandy Brae, which starts as a small road and becomes a rough track.
- **Tollymore Forest Park:** apparently this was the location for the Haunted Forest where the white walkers began their march into the realms of men. If you want to try to spot a direwolf, then try Walks 5, 6 or 10 which all enter the forest.
- **Leitrim Lodge:** the hills in this area provided the landscape for Bran Stark's flight north of Winterfell. Walks 16, 17 and 18 all pass nearby.

The Silent Valley Reservoir

When to go

Usually, you can walk in the Mournes at any time of year. Even in winter there is rarely snow in sufficient quantities to prevent normal hill walking. Each season has plenty to commend it.

Spring (March to May): this can be the most beautiful time of year for walking. Many wildflowers are on show including daffodils, rhododendrons and primroses. The gorse will also be in full bloom with its vivid yellow flowers and coconut aroma. By May, new growth will be upon the larches and other deciduous plants and the weather is often sunny and warm. Indeed, May can be the finest month in Ireland. Visibility in spring is generally excellent so views are wide-ranging. Of course, rain is still a possibility at this time of year but it usually decreases as the season progresses.

Summer (June to August): This is the peak walking season and visitor numbers are at their greatest. Yet when compared to more frequented regions like the Lake District, the Mournes rarely seem busy. Temperatures are at their peak, however, there is sometimes haze. Summer also sees the heather in full bloom, covering the mountains with a beautiful purple carpet.

Autumn (September to November): Holiday makers are generally back at work and schools have started so the Mournes are quieter, particularly mid-week when they often seem deserted. However, autumn sometimes provides the best walking conditions. The weather in September and October tends to be more settled, with less rain than in summer. Temperatures are lower but still comfortable. Skies can be very clear giving excellent visibility and the quality of the low light is magnificent. The wide variety of deciduous plants in Northern Ireland means that the autumn colours are stunning. However, as the days get shorter, it is wise to start walking early. If something were to go wrong, you would have less daylight in which to seek help than in summer.

Month	Pros	Cons
Spring	Pleasant temperatures Frequent sunny skies Good visibility Gorse and wildflowers Fewer visitors	Rainy spells are common in March and April Ground can be wet
Summer	Generally reliably fine weather Heather season	Sometimes hazy Visitor numbers highest
Autumn	Pleasant temperatures Frequent sunny skies Excellent visibility Fewer visitors Autumn colours	Shorter days Cooler evenings
Winter	Sometimes crisp clear skies Excellent visibility Fewer visitors	Shortest days Can be cold and icy Occasionally, there is snow

Winter (December to February): These are the coldest months and although snow can fall on the high peaks, these days heavy snow is not that common. A light sprinkling of snow in the Mournes can be a delight for a suitably equipped walker although care should be taken. However, walking in deep snow is best left to those with the appropriate winter mountain experience and the correct equipment. Even if there is no snow, watch out for ice which forms in the many places where water collects. Cold months often bring crisp clear weather and the low sun makes the light very beautiful. A sunny day in winter can be one of the best of the year. Days are short so start early.

Where to base yourself

The main town in the Mournes is Newcastle which is on the NE edge of the range. Newcastle is a seaside town which is popular with holidaymakers in the summer, and on bank holidays, but is otherwise generally fairly quiet. It is overlooked by Slieve Donard, Northern Ireland's highest peak and so the beauty and tranquillity of the mountains can be appreciated from the town itself. From Newcastle, all of the walks in this book can be easily accessed by car and a number of them can actually be started from the town itself. Newcastle is well served by accommodation and restaurants and in the surrounding countryside, there is plenty of bed and breakfast accommodation. Tourist information is found at the Newcastle Visitor Centre (10-14 Central Promenade, Newcastle; +44 (0)28 4372 2222) or online at www.visitmournemountains.co.uk or www.discovernorthernireland.com.

The seaside town of Newcastle

Using this Book

The walks in this book are only a taste of the many possibilities available in this amazing region. Routes could be shortened or lengthened to meet your needs. Walks have been graded easy, medium, hard or very hard. This is a fairly subjective system (one person's hill is another person's mountain) but you will soon get used to the grading. If there is difficult terrain or significant exposure on a walk then this can impact its categorisation. The route summary table on pages 23 to 25 can help you choose a walk.

In this book:

Timings indicate the time required for a reasonably fit walker to complete the walk. They do not include any stoppage time. Do not get frustrated if your times do not match those given here: everybody walks at different speeds. You will soon learn how your times compare to ours and you will be able to adjust your planning accordingly.

Walking distances are given in both miles and kilometres (km) but road distances are given in miles only. This is because road signs in the UK use miles but Northern Irish mapping grids use kilometres (km). One mile equates to approximately 1.6km.

Place names in brackets in the route descriptions indicate the direction to be followed on signposts. For example, "('Newcastle')" would mean that you follow a sign for Newcastle.

Ascent or descent numbers are the aggregate of all the altitude gain or loss (measured in metres) on the uphill or downhill sections of a route. As a rule of thumb, a fit walker climbs 300 to 400m in an hour.

Elevation profiles tell you where the climbs and descents fall on the route. The profile lines have been deliberately drawn in varying thickness purely for aesthetic purposes. Read the elevations off the top of the lines.

The following abbreviations are used:

MW	Mourne Wall
TL	Turn left
TR	Turn right
SH	Straight ahead
N, S, E and W, etc.	North, South, East and West, etc.

Big Six refers to the six mountains in the range which are higher than 700m: Slieve Donard (849m), Slieve Commedagh (765m), Slieve Binnian (747m), Slieve Bearnagh (739m), Slieve Meelbeg (708m) and Slievelamagan (704m). Occasionally, you may hear people refer to the 'Seven Sevens' because older maps stated that Slieve Meelmore was also higher than 700m. However, current maps indicate that Meelmore is only 687m so we refer to the 'Big Six' instead.

Real maps are provided. These are extracts from OSNI's Activity Map: the Mournes (1:25,000). The routes of the walks are marked on the maps in various different colours. In each walk description, the number of the relevant map and the colour of the route is indicated.

Grid references are provided for the start points of each walk. Please note that 'IG' stands for 'Irish Grid'.

Accommodation

Newcastle lies in the shadow of Slieve Donard, Northern Ireland's highest peak

Accommodation is plentiful in the Mournes. During the busy summer period, or during public holidays, it is wise to book ahead. Outside of these times, you should have no problems finding a beautiful place to stay.

Hotels: Most of the region's hotels are to be found in Newcastle. All will provide breakfast which is usually a cooked offering known as the 'Ulster Fry': a whopping great helping of bacon, sausage, eggs, mushrooms, soda bread and black pudding. Most hotels also offer evening meals. For those with deep pockets, the Slieve Donard Hotel and Spa is a slice of true luxury (www.hastingshotels.com; +44 (0) 28 4372 1066). An easy way of finding and comparing hotels is to use one of the usual travel booking sites such as expedia.com or booking.com: we find the latter to be excellent for the Mournes.

Bed & Breakfast (B&Bs): Normally, bedrooms are basic but clean and comfortable. As with hotels, breakfast will often involve an Ulster Fry. B&Bs can be found and compared using one of the usual travel booking sites such as booking.com. Quality varies but these days most have their own websites to help you make a choice.

Hostels/Lodges: These offer beds in dormitories and often private rooms. Generally, they will have kitchen facilities and communal areas. Hostels in the area include Hutt Hostel (www.hutthostel.com; +44 (0)28 4372 2133) which is well located near the centre of Newcastle and the beach. For something slightly more upmarket and rural, there are a few lodges located out in the heart of the mountains: Meelmore Lodge (www.meelmorelodge.co.uk; +44 (0)28 4372 6657) which is near to the Trassey Track; and the Mourne Lodge (www.themournelodge.com; +44 (0)28 4176 5859) which is close to the Silent Valley.

Campsites: there are a few excellent campsites including one at the Mourne Lodge (see above), which has lovely grassy pitches facing Slieve Meelmore, and one in Tollymore Forest Park (+44 (0)28 4372 2428).

Getting There

Beautiful farmland on Walk 8

The Mourne Mountains are situated just north of the border between Northern Ireland and the Republic of Ireland and so they can be easily accessed from both countries. Newcastle, County Down is the main town in the Mournes.

By air: there are regular flights to Belfast and Dublin from most UK airports and major European cities. There are also flights to Dublin from many US destinations. Airlines using the airports include:

- Belfast City Airport (1hr to Newcastle): British Airways, FlyBe, Air Lingus
- Belfast International Airport (1hr to Newcastle): easyjet, Jet 2, Ryanair
- Dublin Airport (1:40 to Newcastle): Aer Lingus, British Airways, Ryanair, FlyBe, American Airlines, United Airlines, Air Canada

From Belfast City Airport and Belfast International Airport, there are regular buses into Belfast city centre. Taxis are plentiful from both airports. From Belfast city centre, there are frequent buses to Newcastle and Newry (which is also close to the Mournes). From Dublin Airport there are hourly buses to Newry.

From Newry, there are regular buses to Newcastle. Or you could take a taxi. For further information on timetables and routes see www.translink.co.uk.

However, it can be more convenient to rent a car from the airport: approximate driving times to Newcastle are given above. Most of the major car rental companies are represented at each airport but often the best prices can be found on one of the generic car rental booking sites such as www.autoeurope.co.uk or www.holidayautos.co.uk. These websites search all of the options at any particular location and enable you to choose between a variety of rental companies with one search.

By bus or train: From Belfast city centre, there are frequent buses to Newcastle and Newry. From Newry, it is easy to access Newcastle by bus or taxi. A regular train service also runs between Belfast and Dublin, stopping at Newry.

By boat: You can easily bring your car to Ireland from England, Scotland, Wales or France using one of the many ferry services. At the time of writing, the following services are in operation:

Stenaline (www.stenaline.co.uk): Cairnryan/Belfast; Liverpool/Belfast; Holyhead/Dublin; Fishguard/Rosslare; Cherbourg/Rosslare

P&O (www.poferries.com): Cairnryan/Larne; Liverpool/Dublin

Irish Ferries (www.irishferries.com): Holyhead/Dublin; Cherbourg/Dublin; Cherbourg/Rosslare; Roscoff/Rosslare

Approximate drive times to Newcastle from the ports are as follows: Belfast (1hr), Larne (1hr20min), Dublin (1hr45min) and Rosslare (3hr40min).

Granite from local quarries was used to build the MW (Walk 8)

Getting Around

The track at Carrick Little (Walks 25, 26, 27 & 29)

Depending upon where you base yourself, you may be able to access some of the walks in this book by foot: Walks 1, 3 and 4 start from Newcastle itself. For the most part, however, you will need transport to get to the starting points.

From May to August, Translink runs the excellent Mourne Rambler service which is a hop on/hop off bus passing near most of the walk starts. Occasionally, the bus stops are a short walk away from the exact starting point. It runs five times a day (excluding Mondays) from Newcastle bus station, in an anti-clockwise direction, stopping at:

- Bloody Bridge (Walk 2)
- Tollymore Forest Park (Walks 5 and 6)
- Trassey Road (Walks 7, 10, 11 and 12): Trassey Track is ¾mile from the stop
- Moyad Road (Walk 8): Happy Valley car park is ½mile from the stop
- Ott Mountain car park (Walks 9 and 13)
- Spelga Dam (Walk 14)
- Bann's Road car park (Walks 19 and 20)
- Attical (Walks 21 and 22)
- Silent Valley (Walks 23 and 24)
- Carrick Little car park (Walks 25, 26, 27 and 29)
- Rourkes Park (Walk 28)

Using the service, you could catch an early bus from Newcastle to the starting point of your walk and then catch a later bus back to Newcastle when you have finished. It also makes the linear Brandy Pad Traverse (Walk 12) an easier proposition. If you were feeling particularly energetic, it would also be possible to use the service to complete two walks in one day. A day ticket is cheap and allows you to hop on and off as many times as you like. Timetables and route maps for the service can be found at www.translink.co.uk or from the Newcastle Tourist Office.

Alternatively, the Mourne Shuttle Service (www.mourneshuttle.co.uk; +44 (0)7516 412076) offers a year-round bespoke set-down and pick-up service. It also has scheduled shuttle services in the summer months.

A number of taxi companies also operate pick-up and drop-off services which can be good value for groups of two or more. Companies that offer this service include Shimna Taxis (+44 (0)28 4372 3030) and Donard Taxis (+44(0)28 4372 2823).

On the Trail

Weather

The Island of Ireland is known as the 'Emerald Isle' for good reason and its beautiful greenery requires plenty of water. This water is of course supplied by rain and Ireland's location right on the edge of the Atlantic Ocean ensures that there is plenty of it: the island bears the brunt of many Atlantic fronts as they make their way eastwards. Fortunately however, the Mournes are to the E of the island and are therefore not as inclement as the mountains further W such as those in County Kerry: there are plenty of fine days.

As with any mountain region, conditions can change rapidly and the Mourne Mountain Rescue Service gets plenty of business each year from those who get caught out. It is prudent therefore for the walker to be prepared for bad weather and low visibility. All mountains can be dangerous places and need to be treated with respect and caution even if the weather forecast is favourable.

Always get a weather forecast before setting out. Many internet sites provide forecasts, with a varying degree of reliability. The UK Met Office (www.metoffice.gov.uk) is one of the most reliable as it provides regularly updated localised forecasts for different places in the Mournes. It also provides, free of charge, an excellent smartphone app that gives local forecasts.

Maps

The best sheet maps for walking in the Mournes are OSNI's Activity Map: the Mournes (1:25,000) and Harvey's Superwalker Mourne Mountains (1:25,000). The OSNI map is used for all the route maps in this book. It should be noted that occasionally, altitudes on the Harvey map differ slightly from those on the OSNI map. The altitudes in this book are taken, where possible, from the OSNI map.

Paths and Waymarking

In the Mournes, do not assume that your entire route will use clearly defined paths and tracks. As is typical on the Island of Ireland, often there are sections without paths over grass, heather or peat bog. Fortunately, the MW and other dry-stone walls regularly assist with navigation. Signs and waymarks are rare but this is not usually a problem given the presence of the walls. Navigation skills can be useful on some walks.

If you see mountain biking signs, then take care: mountain bikes are fast and often quiet and a collision between a walker and a mountain bike could be serious.

What to take

Ensure that you are properly equipped for the worst terrain and the worst weather conditions that you could encounter: rain, cold and possibly snow. Being cold and wet at altitude is unpleasant and can be dangerous. However, the dilemma is that you should also consider weight and avoid carrying anything unnecessary. The heavier your pack, the harder the climbs will be. Be ruthless as every gram counts.

Fortunately, modern gear helps with this dilemma: there is some fantastic lightweight kit available now. For example, I recently upgraded a backpack, obtaining a weight saving of 600g (almost 10% of overall pack-weight). When choosing gear, check the weights of the different products as the differences can be great.

Layering of clothing is the key to warmth. Do not wear cotton: it does not dry quickly and gets cold.

Recommended Basic Kit

Boots/Shoes	Good quality, properly fitting and worn in. It is fashionable these days to hike with trail running shoes but we prefer boots with ankle support and cleated soles (such as Vibram).	
Socks	Good quality, quick drying walking socks. Wash them regularly and change them daily, helping to avoid blisters.	
Gaiters	A necessity in the Mournes outside of summer: the ground is often wet and boggy.	
Waterproof jacket and trousers	Waterproof and breathable. Some people do not bother with waterproof trousers but we like to carry light ones just in case.	
Base layers	T-shirts and pants of man-made fabrics or merino wool which wick moisture away from your body.	
Fleeces	Man-made fabrics.	
Trousers	The Mournes can be windy so we like softshell trousers for cold weather walking. In warmer weather, lighter walking trousers will suffice.	
Warm hat and gloves	Carry these in all seasons just in case.	
Rucksack	Well padded shoulder straps and waist band. Much of the weight of the pack should sit on your hips rather than your shoulders.	
Waterproof Pack Liner	Rucksacks are not very waterproof. A liner will keep your gear dry if it rains.	
Whistle	For emergencies. Many rucksacks have one incorporated into the sternum strap.	

Head-torch with spare batteries	It is prudent to carry a head torch for emergencies. This can help you get down the mountain safely if you get caught out late and enables you to signal to emergency services.	
Basic first aid kit	Including plasters, a bandage and antiseptic wipes.	
Map and compass	For maps see above. A GPS unit or smartphone apps can be a useful addition but they are no substitute for a map and compass: after all, batteries can run out and electronics can fail.	
Sunglasses, sun hat, sunscreen and lip salve	Sun in the mountains can be brutal, even on the Island of Ireland.	
Walking poles	These transfer weight from your legs onto your arms keeping you fresher. They also save your knees, particularly on descents and can reduce the likelihood of falling or twisting an ankle.	
Phone	A smart phone is a very useful tool on a walking trip. It can be used for emergencies and apps for weather, mapping and hotel booking are invaluable. It can also replace your camera to save weight.	
Space blanket or emergency bag	Very light but it could save your life.	
Food	Carry some emergency food over and above your planned daily ration. Energy bars, nuts and dried fruit are all good.	
Water	Start each day with at least 1.5 litres of water per person. Hydration packs with tubes facilitate more effective hydration by enabling drinking on the move.	

The turret on the summit of Slieve Donard

Safety

The Mourne Wall was built to last

On a calm summer's day the mountains are paradise. But a sudden weather shift or an injury can change things dramatically so treat them with respect and be conscious of your experience levels and physical capabilities. The following is a non-exhaustive list of recommendations:

* The fitter you are at the start of your trip, the more you will enjoy the walking
* Before you set out each day, study the route and make plans based upon the abilities of the weakest member of your party
* Get a weather forecast (daily if possible) and reassess your plans in light of it. Avoid exposed routes if the weather is uncertain
* Start early to avoid ascending during the hottest part of the day and to allow more surplus time in case something goes wrong
* Bring a map and compass and know how to use them
* It can be sensible to call ahead to your accommodation and tell them what time you will arrive. If you do not turn up then they can raise the alarm
* Carry surplus food and clothing for emergencies
* Never be too proud to turn back if you find the going too tough or if the weather deteriorates
* Do not stray from the route so as to avoid getting lost and to help prevent erosion of the landscape
* Avoid exposed high ground in a thunderstorm. If you get caught out in one then drop your walking poles and stay away from trees, overhanging rocks, metal structures and caves. Generally accepted advice is to squat on your pack and keep as low as possible
* In the event of an accident, move an injured person into a safe place and administer any necessary first aid. Keep the victim warm. Establish your exact coordinates and, if possible, use your cell phone to call for help. The emergency number is 999. If you have no signal then send someone for help
* Mountain biking is now popular in the Mournes so watch out. A collision with a bike would not be pleasant

General Information

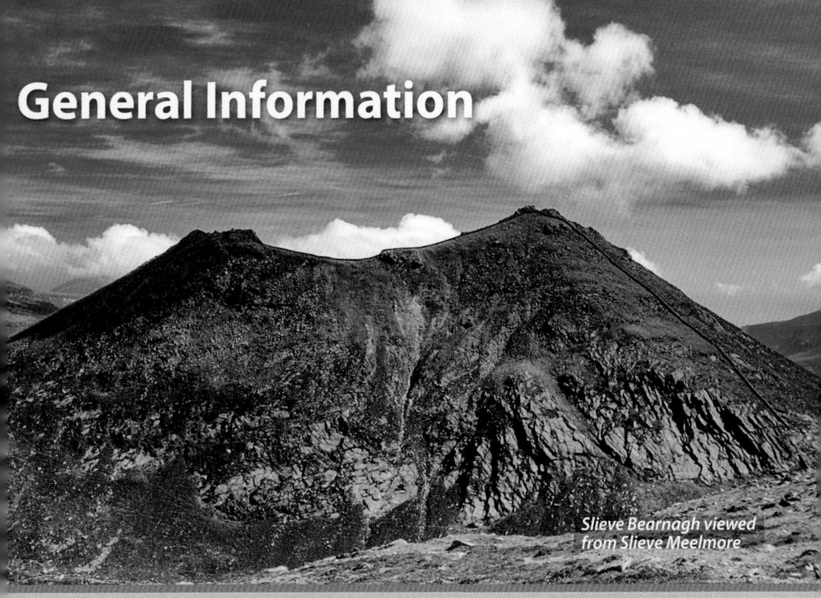

Slieve Bearnagh viewed from Slieve Meelmore

Language: English is the main language.

Charging electronic devices: the UK uses a 3-pin plug.

Money: Northern Ireland uses Sterling (£). ATMs can be found in most towns and in many service stations but rarely in smaller villages. Credit cards are accepted almost everywhere.

Visas: the Mournes are in Northern Ireland which is part of the UK. However, Dublin is in the Republic of Ireland so if you arrive there, you will have to travel overland across the Ireland/UK border into Northern Ireland: you will therefore need to consider the immigration requirements of both the Republic of Ireland and the UK. Citizens of the European Union do not currently need a visa to enter either Ireland or the UK. However, the UK has voted to leave the EU in 2019 and, at the date of publication, it is unclear how this will impact immigration requirements for EU citizens entering the UK. Currently, citizens of Australia, New Zealand, Canada and the US do not need a visa for short tourist trips to Ireland or the UK.

Cell phones: these should work in most towns and villages. In the mountains, however, it can be difficult to get a signal.

International dialling codes: the country code for the UK is +44. For Ireland it is +353. In both cases, you omit the first 0 in the area code if dialling from overseas.

Wifi: nearly all hotels and B&Bs have wifi.

Emergencies and Mountain Rescue: Mourne Mountain Rescue Service is a charity financed by grants and public donations. Its services are free and are provided by unpaid volunteers. The emergency number is 999: ask for Mountain Rescue.

Insurance: it is wise to have adequate insurance which covers hiking. Visitors from the EU should currently be entitled to free (or partly free) medical treatment: any rescue costs would not be covered. However, with Brexit looming this may change for EU citizens and in such circumstances, private insurance will become even more important.

Wildlife & Plants

The bright yellow gorse blooms in spring

Wildlife

In the mountains themselves, mammals (other than sheep) are few and far between: you are much more likely to spot an animal in the surrounding hedgerows and forests. In these areas, the fauna is similar to that in other parts of Ireland or the UK. There are deer, foxes, badgers, rabbits, squirrels, hedgehogs, mice and shrews. There are also hares in Ireland but these are quite rare nowadays. Tollymore Forest Park has one of the largest remaining colonies of red squirrels on the Island of Ireland. Otters are present in the rivers nearby.

Much of the bird life is also similar to that in other parts of Ireland or the UK. Magpies and crows are ubiquitous as are many of the usual species of small birds. Thankfully, buzzards are now quite common again after a difficult 20th century. Jays, ravens, pheasants, grouse and a variety of wild foul can also be seen. However, it is on a coastal walk (such as Walk 30) where you tend to see the most interesting birds: oyster-catchers, terns, gannets, curlews, herons and cormorants are all regularly spotted.

Keen twitchers will be interested to know that Strangford Lough (which is only a short distance away) is one of the finest bird sanctuaries in Europe. As well as many other species, 95% of the world's population of Canadian Light-bellied Brent Geese are thought to be present here in autumn. Strangford Lough also has more than 2000 marine species and 28 of those are found nowhere else in the world.

Plants and flowers

Like many other mountainous places on the Island of Ireland, the peaty soil of the Mourne Mountains is not particularly fertile. In the forests, the most common trees include ash, beech, birch and oak. Larch trees are also common but sadly, the emergence of Japanese larch disease in the area has resulted in the felling of large sections of larch forest. Evidence of this devastation can be seen from the Trassey Track.

Heather is everywhere and when it flowers in summer, the slopes of the mountains take on a gorgeous purple hue. Gorse (or 'Whins' as it is known locally) is also widespread and its yellow flowers are a dominating feature of the Mourne countryside in spring. Anyone who walks through a section of bright gorse will be struck by the mouth-watering coconut aroma.

Sphagnum Moss with its pink or green colours is to be found wherever it is very damp, as is Bog Myrtle, Bog Asphodel and Bog Cotton. The latter is easily spotted in summer with its fluffy white head. The colourful Rhododendron, an imposter, is common around the fringes of the mountains but not in the vast quantities which plague the indigenous plants in the west of Ireland.

Geology

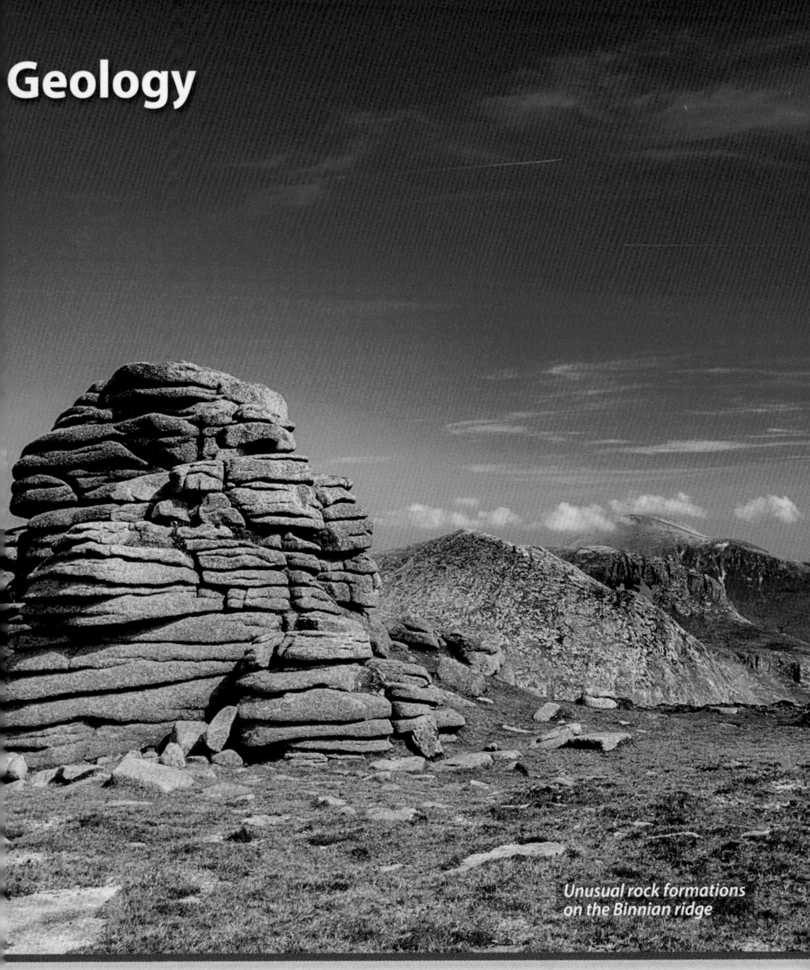

Unusual rock formations on the Binnian ridge

Granite dominates the visible geology of the Mourne Mountains but this is underlain by Silurian rocks of shales, mudstones or greywackes. These are thought to have formed more than 400 million years ago, from mud, sands and silts lying at the bottom of the ocean.

The granites themselves are relative youngsters having developed only 56 million years ago, during a period of high volcanic activity, when the great continents moved apart leaving what is now the NE Atlantic Ocean.

The mountains formed out of molten magma from the earth's centre. The molten rock bubbled up inside the earth's crust and slowly cooled underneath the overlying sandstone to form the interlocking crystals of quartz, feldspar and mica that comprise granite. The granite mountains were formed when blocks of Silurian shale collapsed, leaving a cavity which was filled by an up-welling of acid magma. However, it probably took millions of years and many ice ages to scour and weather the earth to reveal the granite fully. Once revealed, the granite would have been further carved and shaped over the last 2 million years by ice and the weather to produce the mountains that we enjoy today. Evidence of the glacial erosion can be clearly seen in the U-shaped valleys, corries and moraines of the range.

Irish Place Names

Grooves in this granite slab show how the masons split the rock

Many of the mountains and places in this book have Irish names. The translation of these is a challenge as historians often disagree about spellings and meanings. The problems with spellings mainly arise because early English speaking cartographers are likely to have written down many names phonetically from the spoken forms: the Irish pronunciation of consonants and vowels frequently differs from English pronunciations. A list of Irish place names for the Mournes, and their probable English translations, is set out below. Take the translations with a pinch of salt. They have been derived from a number of sources but there may be experts amongst you who disagree.

Name	Meaning in English
Annalong	Ford of long ships
Ben Crom	Stooped peak
Carn	Cairn
Carrick Little	Little rock
Cloghmore	Big stone
Finlieve	White mountain
Leitrim	Grey ridge
Lough Shannagh	Lake of the foxes
Moolieve	Bare mountain
Seefin	Finn's seat
Shanlieve	Old mountain
Slieve Bearnagh	Broken mountain
Slieve Binnian	Mountain of the little horns
Slieve Commedagh	Mountain of watching/look-out
Slieve Corragh	Rugged mountain
Slieve Donard	Mountain of St. Donairt
Slievelamagan	Creeping mountain
Slieve Meelbeg	Mountain of the little ants (or possibly animals)
Slieve Meelmore	Mountain of the big ants (or possibly animals)
Slievemoughanmore	(possibly) Mountain of the great booley (whatever that means!)
Slieve Muck	Mountain of the pigs
Slievenamiskan	Butter dish mountain
Slievenaglogh	Mountain of the rocks
Tievedockaragh	Steep slope

Walk No	Walk Name	Start	Grade	Time	Distance (km)	Distance (miles)	Total Ascent (m)	Total Ascent (ft)	Maximum Altitude (m)	Maximum Altitude (ft)
1	Slieve Donard from Newcastle	Newcastle	Hard	4:10	11.4	7.1	920	3019	849	2786
2	Slieve Donard from Bloody Bridge	Bloody Bridge car park	Hard	4:30	12	7.5	860	2822	849	2786
3	Slieve Commedagh & the Slievenamaddy Ridge	Newcastle	Hard	4:00	10.5	6.5	765	2510	765	2510
4	Donard Forest & Drinnahilly	Newcastle	Easy	2:00	7	4.4	315	1034	254	833
5	Tollymore Forest Park: the Grand Tour	Tollymore Forest Park	Medium	4:00	14.4	8.9	460	1509	240	787
6	Tollymore Forest Park: the River Loop	Tollymore Forest Park	Easy	1:30	5.7	3.5	120	394	136	446
7	Slieve Bearnagh	Trassey Track	Medium	3:15	9.8	6.1	580	1903	739	2425
8	Slieve Meelmore Circuit	Happy Valley car park	Medium	3:45	9.3	5.8	535	1755	687	2254
9	The Meelbeg Ridge	Ott Mountain car park	Hard	4:30	11	6.8	660	2165	708	2323
10	Slieve Commedagh Diamond Circuit	Trassey Track car park	Hard	4:30	13.9	8.6	815	2674	765	2510

Walk No	Walk Name	Start	Grade	Time	Distance (km)	Distance (miles)	Total Ascent (m)	Total Ascent (ft)	Maximum Altitude (m)	Maximum Altitude (ft)
11	The High Mournes Epic Circuit	Trassey Track car park	Hard	5:45	16.7	10.4	1060	3478	849	2786
12	The Brandy Pad Traverse	Trassey Track car park	Medium	4:20	11.9	7.4	440	1444	556	1824
13	Tour of Spelga Dam	Ott Mountain car park	Very Hard	6:00	15.4	9.6	1050	3445	674	2211
14	Butter Mountain Horseshoe	Spelga Dam car park	Easy	2:00	4.8	3.0	210	689	504	1654
15	Hen Mountain	Sandbank Road car park	Easy	1:15	3	1.9	230	755	361	1184
16	Western Mournes Nine Peak Circuit	Sandbank Road car park	Very Hard	7:00	17.1	10.6	1255	4118	638	2093
17	Pierces Castle & Rocky Mountain	Leitrim Lodge car park	Medium	3:40	11.5	7.1	530	1739	467	1532
18	Slievemoughanmore & Rocky River Valley	Leitrim Lodge car park	Hard	4:00	10.2	6.3	640	2100	559	1834
19	Doan & Carn Circuit	Banns Road car park	Medium	4:45	14.6	9.1	530	1739	594	1949
20	Slievenaglogh	Banns Road car park	Medium	2:15	7.1	4.4	251	824	445	1460

Walk No	Walk Name	Start	Grade	Time	Distance (km)	Distance (miles)	Total Ascent (m)	Total Ascent (ft)	Maximum Altitude (m)	Maximum Altitude (ft)
21	The Pigeon Rock Ridge	Attical	Hard	5:00	16	9.9	710	2330	559	1834
22	Eagle Mountain	Attical	Medium	3:40	11.9	7.4	540	1772	638	2093
23	Slieve Bearnagh & the Silent Valley	Silent Valley Mountain Park	Very Hard	7:00	22.4	13.9	790	2592	739	2425
24	Moolieve & the Binnians	Silent Valley Mountain Park	Hard	4:45	11.7	7.3	870	2854	747	2451
25	The Annalong Horseshoe	Carrick Little car park	Very Hard	7:00	19.9	12.4	1220	4003	747	2451
26	Slievelamagan & the Annalong Valley	Carrick Little car park	Hard	5:30	16	9.9	840	2756	704	2310
27	Slieve Binnian & Blue Lough	Carrick Little car park	Medium	3:45	11.7	7.3	710	2330	747	2451
28	Chimney Rock & the Seefins	Quarter Road near Annalong	Hard	4:15	10.1	6.3	710	2330	656	2152
29	The Mourne Wall Epic	Carrick Little car park	Very Hard	12–13	33.4	20.8	2970	9745	849	2786
30	Murlough National Nature Reserve	Twelve Arches car park	Easy	1:45	6	3.7	40	131	19	62

Incredible views of Slieve Binnian and the Silent Valley from the summit of Doan (Walk 19).

Route Descriptions

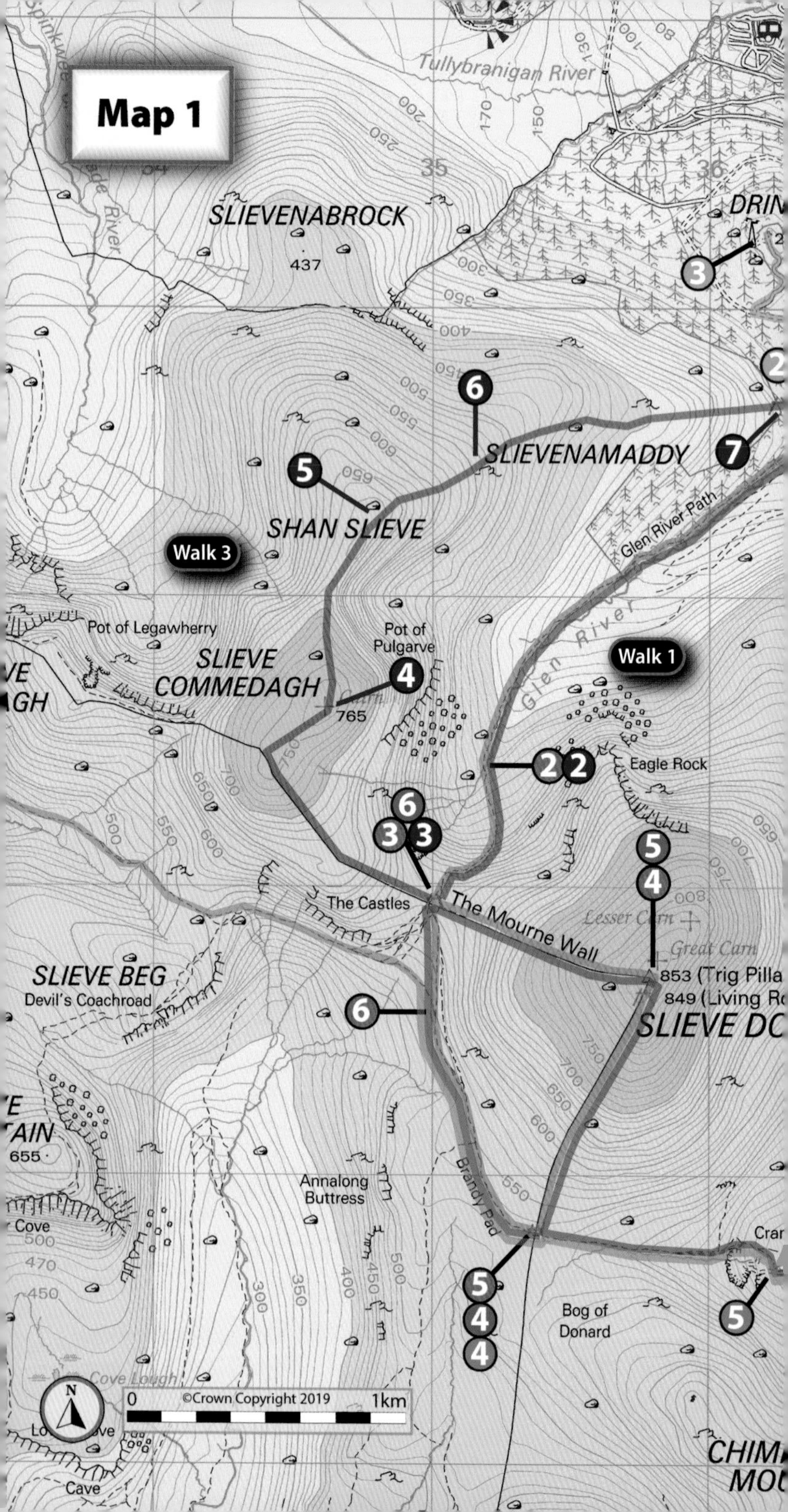

Map 1
Tullybranigan River
SLIEVENABROCK
437
SLIEVENAMADDY
SHAN SLIEVE
Walk 3
Glen River Path
Pot of Legawherry
SLIEVE COMMEDAGH
Pot of Pulgarve
765
Glen River
Walk 1
Eagle Rock
The Castles
The Mourne Wall
Lesser Cairn
Great Cairn
853 (Trig Pilla
849 (Living Ro
SLIEVE DO
SLIEVE BEG
Devil's Coachroad
Annalong Buttress
Brandy Pad
Bog of Donard
Cove
655
Cove Lough
Cave
©Crown Copyright 2019
0
1km
CHIM
MOU

Swimming Pool
Sch
Donard Park
NEWCASTLE
38
39
Black Rock
Swimming Pool
Sch
Sch
Donard Bridge
Police Station
SOUTH PROMENADE
Harbour
Lifeboat Station
Donard Forest
Lindsay's Leap
Stairs
Quarry
Walk 4
KILKEEL ROAD
26
Donard Cove
Drinneevar
460
MILLSTONE MOUNTAIN
Srupatrick
Maggy's Leap
Armor's Hole
Leganabruchan
Shannagh-More Outdoor Education Centre
The Broad Cove
Shannagh-More
Glen Fofanny River
Glen Fofanny
545
Rockabill
Raven Rocks
Sheepfold
Walk 2
Bloody Bridge
FB
Bloody Bridge River
Walk 12
Church
Quarry Track
Mourne Coastal Path
Dulusk Cove
FB
NT
SLIEVENAGARRAGH
452
Sheepfold

The Mourne Wall snaking up to the summit of Slieve Donard from the Bog of Donard

Slieve Donard (from Newcastle)

1

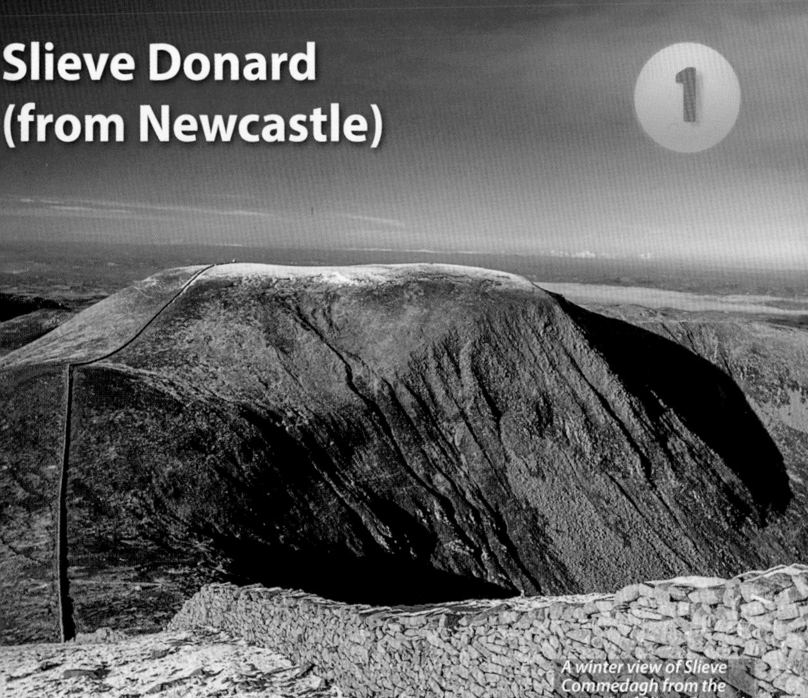

A winter view of Slieve Commedagh from the summit of Slieve Donard

A very fine route up Northern Ireland's highest mountain via the Glen River Path. The views throughout are fantastic. It has the advantage of starting in Newcastle so it makes for a great outing if you are staying there. Due to Slieve Donard's popularity, you are unlikely to be alone on the hills.

The walk is mostly on clear paths although these are sometimes steep and/or uneven underfoot. Part of the walk runs alongside the MW which helps with navigation. Due to the relatively high altitude, this route is best avoided in low visibility.

Time	4:10
Distance	11.4km 7.1 miles
Ascent/Descent	920m 3019ft
Maximum Altitude	849m 2786ft
Grade	Hard
Map	Map No. 1 (red route)

Start/Finish: Donard car park in Newcastle (0m; IG J 374305)

Access: From Newcastle town centre, follow the signs for 'Donard Forest' or 'Donard Car Park' to arrive at the car park at the S side of the town.

The route follows the Glen River on the climb and the descent

S From the S side of the car park, head W along a tarmac driveway. Almost immediately, go through two gates and continue SW on a gravel track. The track soon bears around to the S and narrows to a gravel path which enters woodland and runs uphill alongside the Glen River. After a few minutes, TL and cross the granite **Donard Bridge** which was built in 1835. Immediately afterwards, TR and climb a rocky path with the Glen River just on the right. After a few minutes, at a junction, keep SH to climb some steps. Then, continue uphill alongside the river. Ignore other paths branching off to the left.

1 0:25: TR at a track and cross a large bridge. Immediately afterwards, TL and climb on a rocky path, now with the river on the left. Soon, the path splits but it does not really matter which branch you take as long as you do not stray far from the river. When you arrive at a track, TL and continue to a bridge. Here, take a path heading uphill with the river still on the left. Soon afterwards, pass a 19th century ice house (see Walk 3) on the left and continue climbing on the path, now above the trees. To the SW, you should see the saddle between the peaks of Slieve Donard and Slieve Commedagh. Behind you there are beautiful views of the Irish Sea.

2 1:15: The path fords the river and climbs more steeply.

3 1:30: Arrive at a saddle bisected by the MW (583m): TL and walk uphill (SE) alongside the MW. Alternatively, you can cross the stile over the MW and proceed uphill on its S side: this strategy can pay a warmth dividend depending upon the direction of the wind, however, the N side of the wall is easier underfoot as there are stone steps for much of the climb.

4 2:00: Arrive at the summit of **Slieve Donard (849m)** with its stone turret. This is the highest point in Northern Ireland and the views of the entire Mourne range are magnificent. On a very clear day, the Wicklow Mountains near Dublin can even be spotted to the S. TR and follow the MW downhill (SW) enjoying magnificent views of Slieve Binnian, Slievelamagan and Slieve Bearnagh.

5 2:20: Arrive at a stile over the MW. The path bisecting the wall is the famous Brandy Pad, an old smugglers' route (see Walk 12). Cross the stile and proceed NW on the Brandy Pad. After a few minutes, note the deep chasm in Slieve Beg, the nearest peak to the W: this is the aptly named Devil's Coachroad. 10min from the MW, ignore a path on the right and keep SH on the Brandy Pad: in fact, you could take this path but it is hard going.

6 After another 5min, leave the Brandy Pad for a path on the right heading N towards the saddle you passed earlier (Waypoint no. 3). When you arrive at the saddle, cross the stile and retrace your steps back to the start.

Slieve Donard (from Bloody Bridge)

2

The Mourne Wall guides the way to the summit

No book on the Mournes would be complete without this popular route up Northern Ireland's highest mountain. Due to Slieve Donard's popularity you are unlikely to be alone on the hills.

The walk mostly uses clear paths although these are sometimes steep and/or uneven underfoot. Part of the walk runs alongside the MW which helps with navigation. Due to the relatively high altitude, the walk is best avoided in low visibility.

Time	4:30
Distance	12.0km 7.5 miles
Ascent/Descent	860m 2822ft
Maximum Altitude	849m 2786ft
Grade	Hard
Map	Map No. 1 (blue route)

Start/Finish: Bloody Bridge car park (30m; IG J 389271)

Access: From Newcastle town centre, follow the signs for 'Kilkeel A2'. Head SE out of Newcastle and, after a few miles, arrive at the Bloody Bridge car park on the left.

Follow the Bloody Bridge River on the climb

Fabulous Irish Sea views at Bloody Bridge car park

S From the S side of the car park, cross the road and take a small path beside a National Trust sign, heading W. Do not take the wide track starting to the right of the path. After a few metres, pass through a narrow gap in a fence and descend briefly on a clear path towards the Bloody Bridge River. Soon the path heads uphill with the river on the left. The gorse here is magnificent in spring.

1 0:15: Cross a footbridge and continue uphill, alongside the river, on a rocky path. After a few minutes, cross a stile.

2 0:25: Follow some stone markers ('Mourne Wall') and ford the river on some large boulders. On the other side, continue on a wide track. Shortly afterwards, before a gate, TR and leave the track to climb some stone steps to a stile. Cross the stile and TL onto a path. Shortly afterwards, TR at a junction ('Mourne Wall') and climb a wide track, now heading directly towards Slieve Donard. Soon this track begins to wind back and forth.

3 1:15: Arrive at an old quarry. Look carefully for rocks in which there are man-made grooves: these show how the masons split the rocks with chisels. Follow the path around the right of the quarry and continue upwards to the W. This section is rocky and difficult and the path can be unclear: if in doubt, keep heading W. Eventually, the MW comes into view with Slieve Binnian and Slievelamagan behind.

4 1:30: Arrive at the MW: TR and walk uphill alongside it. The slope gets steeper and steeper.

5 2:10: Finally the slope levels off and you arrive at the summit of **Slieve Donard (849m)**. This is the highest point in Northern Ireland and the views of the entire Mourne range are magnificent. On a very clear day, the Wicklow mountains near Dublin can even be spotted to the S. Cross the stile over the MW and walk downhill (initially W), still alongside the MW.

6 2:40: Arrive at a saddle: TL and follow a path heading initially SE. Soon, arrive at a junction with a clear path snaking away to the NW: this is the famous Brandy Pad (see Walk 12). TL and follow the Brandy Pad back to the MW (Waypoint No. 4; 3hr10min). Climb the stile over the MW and retrace your steps back to the start. When you cross the river at Waypoint no. 2, ensure that you go SH, briefly uphill: do not descend to the right.

The Slievenamaddy ridge seen from the summit of Slieve Commedagh

Ice Houses

Before electricity and fridges made refrigeration widely available, only the rich could afford it through the luxury of an ice house. Mostly these were covered underground chambers, built near to a good natural source of ice such as a lake or a river. In the case of the Donard ice house, ice was brought from the nearby Glen River and the Black Stairs cliffs. The ice would have been placed inside the ice house and packed with straw or sawdust for insulation. It would have remained frozen for many months and often into the summer.

Ice houses began to be recorded in Ireland in the 17th century but they became more prevalent by the mid-19th century, by which time their efficiency had improved dramatically due to advancements in construction techniques.

Slieve Commedagh & the Slievenamaddy Ridge

3

The turret near Slieve Commedagh is one of only three on the entire MW

A wonderful, yet little known, circular route involving Northern Ireland's second highest mountain. Although the first section up the Glen River is busy with walkers climbing Slieve Donard, the remainder of the route is very quiet and if isolation is what you seek then you will find it on the Slievenamaddy Ridge. The walk also has the advantage of starting in Newcastle so it makes for a great outing if you are staying there.

Time	4:00
Distance	10.5km 6.5 miles
Ascent/Descent	765m 2510ft
Maximum Altitude	765m 2510ft
Grade	Hard
Map	Map No. 1 (purple route)

The route is straightforward except for the descent along the Slievenamaddy Ridge where there is no clear path, the ground can be wet and careful navigation is required. Also, just after the summit of Slieve Commedagh, the path runs near the edge of some steep cliffs: best avoided in high winds or low visibility.

Start/Finish: Donard car park in Newcastle (0m; IG J 374305)

Access: From Newcastle town centre, follow the signs for 'Donard Forest' or 'Donard Car Park' to arrive at the car park at the S side of the town.

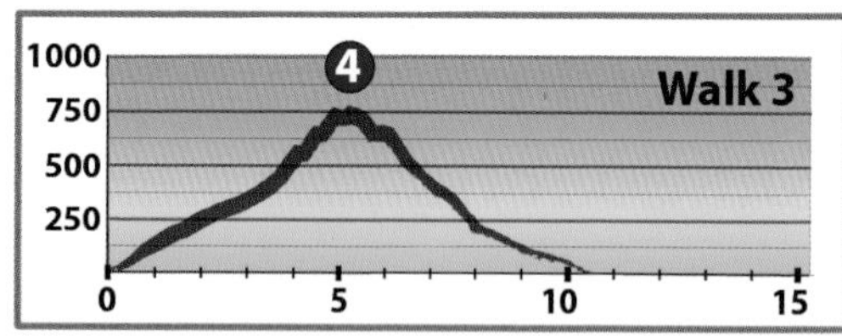

S From the S side of the car park, head W along a tarmac driveway. Almost immediately, go through two gates and continue SW on a gravel track. The track soon bears around to the S and narrows to a gravel path which enters woodland and runs uphill alongside the Glen River. After a few minutes, TL and cross the granite Donard Bridge which was built in 1835. Immediately afterwards, TR and climb a rocky path with the Glen River just on the right. After a few minutes, at a junction, keep SH to climb some steps. Then, continue uphill alongside the river. Ignore other paths branching off to the left.

1 0:25: TR at a track and cross a large bridge. Immediately afterwards, TL and climb on a rocky path, now with the river on the left. Soon, the path splits but it does not really matter which branch you take as long as you do not stray far from the river. When you arrive at a track, TL and continue to a bridge. Here, take a path heading uphill with the river still on the left. Soon afterwards, pass a 19th century ice house on the left (see information box) and continue climbing on the path, now above the trees. To the SW, you should see the saddle between the peaks of Slieve Donard and Slieve Commedagh. Behind you there are beautiful views of the Irish Sea.

2 1:15: The path fords the river and climbs more steeply.

3 1:30: Arrive at a saddle bisected by the MW (583m): TR and climb steeply alongside the MW until you reach a stone turret at the top of the slope. Then walk NE for a few minutes.

4 2:00: Arrive at the summit cairn of **Slieve Commedagh (765m)**. Head N and shortly afterwards, pass a cairn. Arrive near the edge of some cliffs. Do not stray too close to the edge as a fall could have serious consequences. Follow a faint path along the edge of the cliffs.

5 The path passes near a large cairn on the summit of **Shan Slieve (683m)**, overlooking the broad Slievenamaddy Ridge which the route will take you along. Descend NE on a faint path. When the path disappears, keep NE, just to the right of the crest of the ridge. The ground is boggy in places but the heather is wonderful in summer. Eventually, the ridge bends to the right heading E towards a little spur below. Pass a fenced enclosure.

6 After a few minutes, arrive at the spur known as **Slievenamaddy**. Follow a grassy path downwards (SE) for a few metres. Then, TL onto a grassy path and descend NE. After a few minutes, descend steeply through a shallow gully to the right of a rocky outcrop. Towards the foot of the gully, the path bends to the right and heads SE towards Donard Forest.

7 Cross a stile to enter the forest. Immediately afterwards, TR through a fence onto a small path heading initially E down through trees: mountain bikers use this path so take care. There is a labyrinth of paths in the forest: if in doubt, keep heading downhill. Eventually, pass through a gap in a dry-stone wall and head NE through more open forest. Ignore offshoots to the path and continue SH.

8 TL at a track. Soon afterwards, TR at a junction, descending on a track with great views of Newcastle and Murlough National Nature Reserve. At the next junction, TL.

9 After 5min, TR onto another track. After 10min, arrive back at Donard Bridge. TL and retrace your steps to the start.

Donard Forest & Drinnahilly

4

An evening view of Slieve Donard from Drinnahilly

This walk through the lovely Donard Forest may be easy but it still offers fabulous views of the high Mournes. Part of the route is on the 'Granite Trail' which provides a fascinating insight into the lives of the quarry men who worked in the mountains back in the day.

There is little altitude gain or loss so this is a walk for all the family. The route uses clear tracks and paths throughout and poses little difficulty with navigation.

Time	2:00
Distance	7.0km 4.4 miles
Ascent/Descent	315m 1034ft
Maximum Altitude	254m 833ft
Grade	Easy
Map	Map No. 1 (orange route)

Start/Finish: Donard car park in Newcastle (0m; IG J 374305)

Access: From Newcastle town centre, follow the signs for 'Donard Forest' or 'Donard Car Park' to arrive at the car park at the S side of the town.

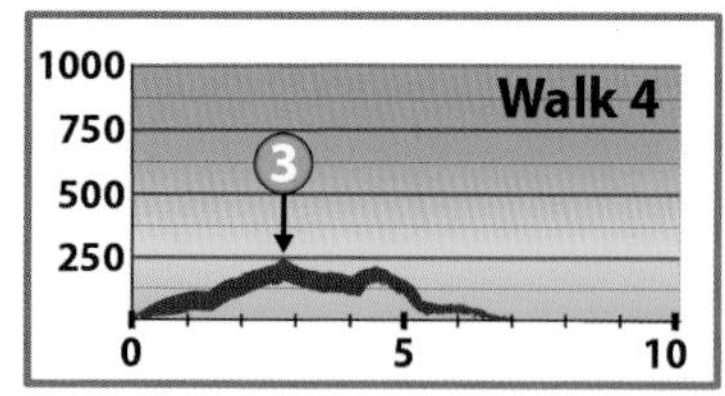

S From the S side of the car park, head W along a tarmac driveway. Almost straight-away, go through two gates and continue SW on a gravel track. The track soon bears around to the S and narrows to a gravel path which enters woodland and runs uphill alongside the Glen River. After a few minutes, arrive at the granite **Donard Bridge** which was built in 1835. Do not cross it but TR and walk up a road (NW). A few metres further on, TL at a junction to continue climbing on the road which soon becomes a forest track. After a minute or so, the track bends to the right and continues gently uphill through deciduous woodland to the NW. Keep on the track past two houses.

1 Shortly afterwards, at a junction, turn sharply left and continue SE on another track. Soon you will get great views of Slieve Commedagh and the slopes of Slieve Donard. After 5min, TR at a junction to head W on a wide gravel track. This track soon bends sharply left and continues climbing. The views of Newcastle and the Irish Sea are superb. Murlough National Nature Reserve (see Walk 30) is visible to the NE.

2 TR at another track (NW). After 5min, TR onto a sealed track.

3 0:45: After another 5min, arrive at the peak of **Drinnahilly (254m)**. From here, retrace your steps to Waypoint no. 2: at the junction, keep SH. After 5min, cross the Glen River on a bridge and keep SH on the track on the other side. After another 5min, the track begins to climb again.

4 1:15: Arrive at a viewpoint with a granite information board. There is also an old quarry here. From the information board, head towards a stile a few metres away to the S. Climb the stile and continue on a path heading downhill (SE). After a few minutes, the path bends to the left and arrives at another stile: cross it and continue on a stone track heading downhill (NE).

5 After 5min, TL onto a track. After another 5min, arrive at a fork: take the track on the right. At the next junction, TR and keep on the main track. At the Glen River, TR and descend alongside it on a rocky path. Soon afterwards, arrive back at Donard Bridge: cross it and TR to retrace your steps to the start.

One of the many beautiful waterfalls in Donard Forest

Foley's Bridge in Tollymore Forest Park

Game of Throne's Haunted Forest?

Tollymore Forest Park: The Grand Tour

Fantastic coastal views from the top of the forest park

This is the longest walk in the lovely Tollymore Forest Park. It travels almost all the way around the perimeter of the park and takes in its high points too. There are stunning views of the high mountains along the entire southern section of the route. The low altitude means that the walk can be undertaken in all seasons. However, the park is perhaps at its best in autumn when the colours of the leaves are a beautiful counterpoint to the greens of the mossy rocks and the crystal clear waters of the streams and rivers.

The route mainly uses wide paths and navigation is straightforward thanks to the excellent waymarking: simply follow black arrows all the way.

Apparently, Tollymore was used in Game of Thrones as the Haunted Forest where the white walkers began their march into the realms of men.

Time	4:00
Distance	14.4km 8.9 miles
Ascent/Descent	460m 1509ft
Maximum Altitude	240m 787ft
Grade	Medium
Map	Map No. 2 (red route)

Start/Finish: Tollymore Forest Park Main Car Park (88m; IG J 345326)

Access: From the centre of Newcastle, follow the signs for 'Bryansford' and 'Tollymore Forest Park'. About 2 miles from the town centre, arrive at the gates of Tollymore Forest Park on left. The car park is about ¾mile from the gate. There is a small charge for use of the car park.

5

S From the information board at the S side of the car park, head W on a tarmac path. A few minutes later, at a junction, TL and cross a footbridge. Descend briefly through deciduous woodland. TR at another path by a wooden cabin.

1 After a few more minutes, at a junction of tracks, TL and descend. At the next junction, ignore a path on the left and continue SH. After another 10-15min, TL at another junction ('King's Grave'). The track loops to the left and shortly afterwards, bends to the right.

2 0:25: Arrive at **Parnell's Bridge**, a beautiful, moss covered, stone bridge which was constructed in 1842. It was the last of the stone bridges to be built in the forest and was named after Sir John Parnell who made many visits here in the 18th century. Immediately before the bridge, TR onto a path which runs alongside the Shimna River. After 5min, cross a wooden footbridge.

3 After another few minutes, the path climbs to a junction. Take the second path on the right. The path climbs to another junction: TL. After 5-10min, TR (W) at the next junction. As you approach the fringes of the forest, there are great views of the high Mournes. Slieve Bearnagh and Slieve Meelmore are the two most prominent peaks. Follow the path around to the left when it reaches a dry-stone wall and continue E. Ignore offshoots to the left and right. The path soon descends back into the forest.

4 TR at another path. As you descend from here, there are tantalising glimpses of Slieve Commedagh. After 5min, TL (NE) at a junction. Shortly afterwards, at another junction, TR on a wide path. Cross **Hore's Bridge** and shortly afterwards, TR at a junction ('Drinns' and 'car park'). After a few more minutes, keep SH at the next junction.

5 Soon afterwards, at another junction, turn hard right (black arrow with white stripe on it). This path climbs to a dry-stone wall with more fantastic views of the high Mournes. Keep uphill on the path alongside the wall: after a while, the path veers away from it.

6 Shortly afterwards, TR at a junction (black arrow with white stripe) and head SE on a wide path. Not long after the junction, TL onto a small grassy path (black arrow with white stripe). After a few minutes, TR at a junction of paths. After a few more minutes, arrive at a beautiful viewpoint: Slieve Donard, Slieve Commedagh and Slieve Meelmore can all be seen. The views of Newcastle and the Irish Sea are also magnificent. There are three lovely stone benches upon which you can rest. From the viewpoint, head S (black arrow with white stripes) to embark upon a stunning but steep descent.

7 TL onto a wide path (black arrow with white stripe). At the next junction, keep SH (black arrow with white stripe).

8 After a few minutes, TL at a fork (black arrow with white stripe). The path climbs through beautiful deciduous forest. After 5-10min, TR at another fork. About 3hr from the start, TR at the junction passed earlier (Waypoint no. 5).

9 After 5-10min, TR at a junction. Shortly afterwards, TL at a fork. After a few more minutes, keep SH at a junction.

10 After 10-15min, TL at a junction. After a few minutes, TR at another path and head downstream alongside the Shimna River. Shortly afterwards, TL to cross **Ivy Bridge**, built in 1780 with elaborate turrets. Immediately after the bridge, turn sharp left and proceed alongside the river again, this time upstream.

11 After 5min, arrive at the magnificent **Foley's Bridge** which was built in 1787 by James Hamilton, 2nd Earl of Clanbrassil. Keep SH, past the bridge, continuing to walk upstream alongside the river. After 5min, arrive at **Old Bridge**, the oldest of the bridges in the park, built in 1726, again by James Hamilton. Beside the bridge there is a complicated junction of paths: take the second path on the right (N). After a few minutes, arrive back at the car park.

Tollymore Forest Park: The River Loop

6

A weir in Tollymore Forest Park

This lovely little walk can be undertaken at any time of year. In autumn, the colours of the changing leaves are truly magnificent and in spring, the bluebells along the route are a sight to behold. The walk takes you on easy paths alongside the Shimna and Cascade rivers whose crystal clear waters gush delightfully over, and around, mossy rocks and boulders. There is little in the way of altitude gain or loss and navigation is straightforward thanks to the fantastic waymarking: simply follow the red arrows. For more information on the park see the introduction section.

Apparently, Tollymore was used in Game of Thrones as the Haunted Forest where the white walkers began their march into the realms of men.

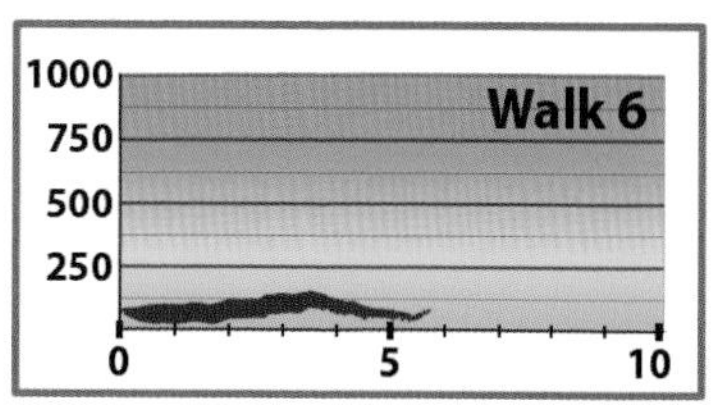

Time	1:30
Distance	5.7km 3.5miles
Ascent/Descent	120m 394ft
Maximum Altitude	136m 446ft
Grade	Easy
Map	Map No. 2 (blue route)

Start/Finish: Tollymore Forest Park Main Car Park (88m; IG J 345326)

Access: From the centre of Newcastle, follow the signs for 'Bryansford' and 'Tollymore Forest Park'. About 2 miles from the town centre, arrive at the gates of Tollymore Forest Park on left. The car park is about ¾mile from the gate. There is a small charge for use of the car park.

Autumn colours in Tollymore Forest Park

S From the car park, head W on a tarmac path. Shortly afterwards, TL. Descend and pass under a beautiful old stone bridge. Immediately afterwards, the path forks: take either fork and descend. After a few minutes, cross over a gravel path and descend S on another gravel path.

1 Soon afterwards, TR at another gravel path and walk upstream alongside the Shimna River. Eventually, arrive at the old **Hermitage** which was built in 1770 by James Hamilton, 2nd Earl of Clanbrassil as a memorial to one of his friends. Back in the day, the lady gentry sheltered in the Hermitage while the gentlemen fished for salmon in the river. Take the left fork to head into the little stone structure and climb the steep stone steps on the other side. TL at the top of the steps and continue along the river.

2 0:40: Arrive at **Parnell's Bridge**, a beautiful, moss covered, stone structure which was constructed in 1842. It was the last of the stone bridges to be built in the forest and was named after Sir John Parnell who made many visits here in the 18th century. TL and cross the bridge. At the other side, TL. Shortly afterwards, at a fork, TR and begin to climb.

3 After 5min, TL at a fork. Lovely views of the high Mournes now appear.

4 At a crossroads, TL and walk down the left bank of the Cascade River.

5 After 5-10min, TR at a junction and cross a bridge. Shortly afterwards, on the left is the confluence of the Cascade and Shimna rivers. After a while, pass the Hermitage again (across the river on the left). From here, you get a good perspective of the structure. Continue SH on the main path.

6 After a few minutes, TL at the next junction. Shortly afterwards, leave the path for a smaller path on the right which runs alongside a beautiful lake. After the lake, keep SH to the NE.

7 Cross **Old Bridge**, the oldest of the bridges in the park, built in 1726 by James Hamilton, 2nd Earl of Clanbrassil. Then continue SH, following the red arrows, to climb back up to the car park.

Slieve Bearnagh

Doan, Carn and Lough Shannagh seen from the summit of Slieve Bearnagh

This route is a Mourne classic. Slieve Bearnagh is the fourth highest mountain in the range and its rocky summit is one of the most recognisable from afar. Given its central position amongst many of the other high peaks, the views from the top on a clear day are special.

The route is relatively short but the terrain is steep in places. The first section of the walk is an easy climb up the rocky Trassey Track. Once you leave the track, paths are sporadic on the climb to the summit and the first section of the descent: these sections are rocky and often steep so take care in the wet.

In low visibility, the summit plateau can be a confusing place and the route passes near a number of steep cliffs so save it for a clear day. In poor conditions, stick close to the MW which acts as a guide from the Hares' Gap to the summit and back down the other side.

Time	3:15
Distance	9.8km 6.1miles
Ascent/Descent	580m 1903ft
Maximum Altitude	739m 2425ft
Grade	Medium
Map	Map No. 3 (red route)

Start/Finish: Trassey Track car park (158m; IG J 311314)

Access: From Newcastle, take the A50 NW towards Castlewellan. After just under 2 miles, TL onto the Ballyhafry Road towards Bryansford. After 2 miles, TL onto the Trassey Road and drive ¾mile to the car park on the left.

Climbing alongside the MW to the summit of Slievenaglogh (Walk 20)

Bridge
Cairn
New
S F
P
263
250
Trassey
Bridge
CLONACHULLION
HILL
230
220
Amenity Area
P
WC
FB
Ford
TRASSEY ROAD
Ford
8
7
Sheepfold
LUK
MOUN
Trassey River
Trassey Track
Sheepfold
Clonachullion
7
Sheepfold
Spellack
Ford
6
1
6
Ford
586
Diamond
Rocks
5
SLIEVE MEELMORE
3
1
5
2
Hares' Gap
Sheepfold
Pollaphuca
Bearnagh
Slabs
3
2
The Mourne Wall
North Tor
5
4
739
Summit Tor
4
SLIEVE
BEARNAGH
4
Blue Lough
SHANNAGH
Shelter
Stone
©Crown Copyright 2019
0
1km
N

Slieve Bearnagh viewed from the Meelbeg Ridge (see Walk 9)

S From the car park, TL and head up the road briefly. Just after a house on the left, go through a farm gate onto the broad Trassey Track. After 10min, go through another gate and continue up the track. Up ahead you will see Slieve Meelmore and behind it Slieve Bearnagh, your destination. Pass through another gate and keep SH on the track.

1 Eventually, cross a stream to arrive at a junction: keep SH (the left fork). Shortly afterwards, TL at another fork. After a few minutes, the sandy track becomes rocky. Keep SH to climb SE up the rocky slope towards a saddle known as the Hares' Gap. The path is intermittent so just work your way upwards SE. Take care on the rocks in the wet.

2 1:00: Climb over the MW using a stile to arrive at the **Hares' Gap (437m)**. At the large cairn, TR and follow a path initially running SW alongside the MW. The path climbs large stone steps to skirt to the left of some steep cliffs. Shortly after the stone steps, the path forks: TR to take the rocky path climbing the slope. There are a number of paths which climb towards the summit: climb SW up the steep slope keeping close to the MW which goes all the way to the top.

3 1:40: Approach the steep cliffs of the **North Tor** of **Slieve Bearnagh (705m)**. Take a clear path which climbs briefly and then skirts to the left (S) of the North Tor, away from the MW. Soon the path heads towards the W. When the path disappears, keep heading W until you arrive close to the MW again. Continue to climb up alongside the MW.

4 1:50: Arrive at the rocky outcrops on the summit of **Slieve Bearnagh (739m)**. The more adventurous might like to scramble the extra few metres up some of the rocks to reach the highest point but take care as the rocks are steep. The other five peaks over 700m can be seen from here: Slieve Commedagh and Slieve Donard to the E; Slievelamagan to the SE; Slieve Binnian to the S; and Slieve Meelbeg to the W. From the summit, follow the path around to the W and descend steeply, keeping close to the MW. Once again, there are a number of available paths but as long as you keep close to the MW you should not go wrong. The steep descent is rocky so watch your footing, particularly in the wet. Do not cross over to the N side of the MW as there are steep cliffs there.

5 Arrive at a saddle with a stile over the MW: cross the stile and continue SH (NE) along a path. When the path becomes faint, keep heading NE. Eventually, arrive at an old stone quarry track: follow this all the way back to the Trassey Track. At the Trassey Track (Waypoint no. 1), TL and retrace your steps to the start.

Sunrise at the Hares' Gap

S From the car park, walk SE uphill alongside a stream. Cross a stile and continue on a track which soon arrives alongside a fence. Shortly after the fence bends to the right, TL at a post with waymarks (onto the Mourne Way): descend briefly and cross a stream on stones. On the other side, cross a stile. Immediately afterwards, walk SE on a faint grassy path heading up into the valley towards a saddle. Soon the path flanks a stream bed which may be dry. At times it is easier to walk up the bed of the stream.

1 0:35: Pass an old quarry and stone shelter. Continue S, and then SE, on a grassy path towards a dry-stone wall. Arrive at the dry-stone wall just where it makes a right-angle turn to the left: climb through a gap in the wall and continue SE up the slope on a faint path.

2 After 5min, cross the MW on a stile and TL to climb alongside it.

3 1:30: Cross a stile by a turret in a corner of the MW. Immediately afterwards, TL and head briefly S to the summit cairn of **Slieve Meelmore (687m)**. Return to the turret and cross the stile again. Then, follow the wall SE downhill. Slieve Bearnagh is prominent to the SE. Towards the bottom of the slope, the rocks are very steep.

4 At a saddle, TL to cross a stile over the MW and continue on a path initially NE. When the path becomes faint, keep heading NE. Eventually the path arrives onto an old quarry track.

5 Shortly after the track bends left (N), leave it for a faint path heading NE across the slope. Soon afterwards, arrive at a quarry where rock was extracted for the MW. Look out for grooves in the rocks made by the quarrymen. Follow the track down to the N.

6 TL onto the wide Trassey Track to head NW down the valley.

7 After 20-30min, TL at a gate and walk alongside a dry-stone wall. For the rest of the route follow Mourne Way waymarks. Ford a couple of streams on rocks. After 30-40min, arrive at the stile crossed previously near the start of the walk: retrace your steps to the start.

Slieve Meelbeg and the MW viewed on the ascent

Slieve Meelmore Circuit

8

The turret in the Mourne Wall near the summit of Slieve Meelmore

A spectacular foray into the high Mournes, following the MW along a ridge to one of the range's highest peaks. There are incredible views of Slieve Binnian and the Silent Valley. Navigation and terrain are generally straightforward.

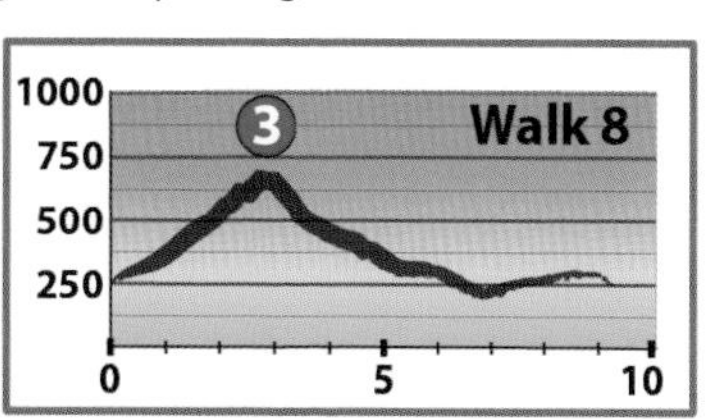

Time	3:45
Distance	9.3km 5.8miles
Ascent/Descent	535m 1755ft
Maximum Altitude	687m 2254ft
Grade	Medium
Map	Map No. 3 (blue route)

Start/Finish: Happy Valley car park (249m; IG J 293297)

Access: From Newcastle, take the A50 NW towards Castlewellan. After just under 2 miles, TL onto the Ballyhafry Road towards Bryansford. After 2 miles, TL onto the Trassey Road and drive 2¼ miles to the Happy Valley car park on the left.

Slieve Bearnagh seen through a gap in the MW

The Meelbeg Ridge

9

Beautiful scenes on the climb to the MW

This fantastic route travels one of the major ridges of the high Mournes. Along the way, three of the range's key peaks are climbed: Slieve Loughshannagh (619m), Slieve Meelbeg (708m) and Slieve Meelmore (687m). The views are spectacular and the ridge is a magnificent place from which to view Slieve Bearnagh, one of the most recognisable peaks in the Mournes. Completing this walk would enable you to tick off one of the Big Six.

The climb to the MW, and the walk along the ridge, pose few difficulties. However, care needs to be taken on the descent from Slieve Meelmore because after Spellack there is a steep, difficult section with no path: you may need to scramble down some rocks. This section also requires careful navigation as there are steep cliffs to the E of Spellack. Navigation on the remainder of the route is straightforward and the MW acts as a navigational aid along the ridge.

Time	4:30
Distance	11.0km 6.8miles
Ascent/Descent	660m 2165ft
Maximum Altitude	708m 2323ft
Grade	Hard
Map	Map No. 3 (green route)

Start/Finish: Ott Mountain car park (379m; IG J 280278)

Access: From Newcastle, take the A50 NW towards Castlewellan. After just under 2 miles, TL onto the Ballyhafry Road (B180) towards Bryansford. Pass through Bryansford and then after 2¼ miles, TL at a junction ('Silent Valley'). After 3½ miles arrive at the car park on the right.

Fofanny Dam

S From the car park, walk down the road (NE) for a few metres. Then, cross the road and a stile beside a gate to pick up a stony path heading SE.

1 After a few minutes, TR at a junction of tracks (following a yellow arrow on a rock). After 25min, when the rocky path ends, continue SH (E) on a muddy path which is faint in places. Keep roughly E, aiming for the MW which is up ahead.

2 0:40: Cross a stile over the MW. Then TL and follow the wall NE. As you climb, you will notice the peaks of Doan and Slieve Binnian on the right. The Silent Valley reservoir soon becomes visible to the S.

3 1:00: Arrive at the top of **Slieve Loughshannagh (619m)**. Keep following the MW: descend to a saddle and then climb up the other side.

4 1:40: Cross the summit of **Slieve Meelbeg (708m)** and continue following the MW as it descends briefly to a saddle. At the saddle, cross a stile to the W side of the MW. Then climb the slope still following the MW. When the MW bisects another dry-stone wall, keep heading uphill (NE).

5 2:10: Pass the summit cairn of **Slieve Meelmore (687m)** and shortly afterwards, reach a stone turret built into a corner of the MW. Leave the MW here and head N along the ridge towards a large stone cairn. From the cairn, head slightly right for a few metres to pick up a faint path. Then walk roughly NE down the crest of the broad ridge.

6 After 20–25min, the path arrives at a rocky outcrop (known as **Spellack**) with a cairn on its left side. The views from the top of Spellack are amazing: Slieve Donard, Slieve Commedagh, Slieve Bearnagh and the Hares' Gap are all clearly visible. Immediately before Spellack, TL on a faint grassy path which quickly disappears. Pick your way down to the NW through a grassy gully. If in doubt, head in the direction of a large lake which can be seen to the NW. Then make for a track below which runs to the NW. The descent is steep in places so take care. Pick your route carefully to avoid the steepest sections and be careful not to stray too far to the right as there are sharp drops. You may find a faint path in places but even so, a bit of light scrambling is required.

7 Eventually, arrive at the track **(IG J 310298)**. Here there is an old quarry from which rocks were extracted to build the MW. You can see parallel grooves in many of the rocks which were used to break them. Follow the track (initially NW).

8 3:10: TL at a dry-stone wall and walk alongside it. For the rest of the route, you can follow waymarks for the Mourne Way.

9 The dry-stone wall ends at a stream. Cross a stile and ford the stream on some rocks. Then proceed on a path on the other side in the direction of a post with waymarks. At the post, TL and head uphill on a rocky path. After a few metres, TR at another post and head along a grassy path.

10 Cross a stile just before **Fofanny Dam**. Shortly afterwards, cross a little bridge to the right. Then proceed S along the left side of the reservoir. After the reservoir, keep following Mourne Way signs along a grassy path which bends around to the right to head towards a forest. At the forest, TL. Soon afterwards, the path heads into the forest and, after a couple of minutes, emerges again at a stile. Cross the stile and TR uphill alongside a fence. After climbing for a few minutes, cross a stile onto a road: TL and walk up the road to return to the car park.

Slieve Commedagh Diamond Route

10

The route traverses an incredible ridge alongside the MW

The goal of this incredible ridge walk is to summit the second-highest peak in the Mournes and it offers some of the finest mountain vistas in Ireland. The long climb to the summit is sublime: you simply follow the MW along the ridge as it snakes upwards, enjoying shimmering Irish Sea views. The author has named the route the 'Diamond Route' not only because it is the finest route up this fantastic mountain, but also because he proposed to his wife here: fortunately, she accepted!

The first half of the walk poses few difficulties. From the Hares' Gap, you follow the MW all the way to the summit so navigation is straightforward. The descent, on the other hand, is quite tricky. Soon after leaving the summit, the path skirts the edge of some high cliffs and, for this reason, the route should be avoided in low visibility. Also, at Shan Slieve the path disappears altogether and for much of the remainder of the walk you will be 'free-styling' across grassy slopes, some of which are very steep. There are also some steep cliffs on the descent which need to be circumvented. Some navigation skills will be useful.

Time	4:30
Distance	13.9km 8.6miles
Ascent/Descent	815m 2674ft
Maximum Altitude	765m 2510ft
Grade	Hard
Map	Map No. 4 (red route)

Start/Finish: Trassey Track car park (158m; IG J 311314)

Access: From Newcastle, take the A50 NW towards Castlewellan. After just under 2 miles, TL onto the Ballyhafry Road towards Bryansford. After 2 miles, TL onto the Trassey Road and drive ¾mile to the car park on the left.

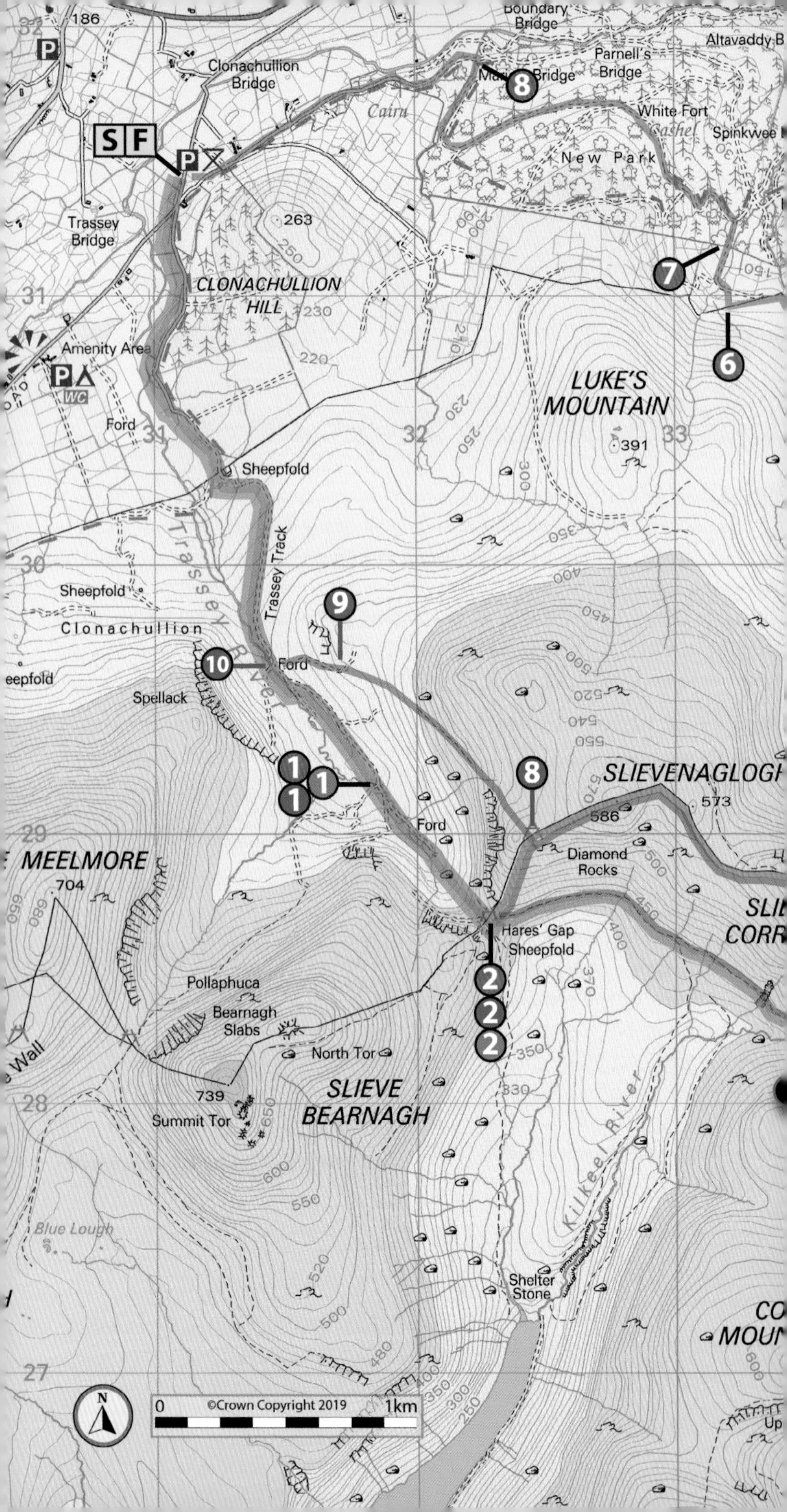

Boundary Bridge
Altavaddy B
Parnell's Bridge
Clonachullion Bridge
Cairn
White Fort
Cashel
Spinkwee
New Park
Trassey Bridge
263
CLONACHULLION HILL
Amenity Area
Ford
LUKE'S MOUNTAIN
391
Sheepfold
Trassey Track
Trassey River
Sheepfold
Clonachullion
Ford
Spellack
SLIEVENAGLOGH
573
586
Ford
Diamond Rocks
MEELMORE
704
Hares' Gap
Sheepfold
Pollaphuca
Bearnagh Slabs
North Tor
SLIEVE BEARNAGH
739
Summit Tor
Kilkeel River
Blue Lough
Shelter Stone
©Crown Copyright 2019
0
1km

Map 4
The Meeting of The Waters
Parnell's View
Tollymore Forest Park
The Drinns
Curraghard
Tullybranigan River
Tipperary Lane
Greenhill (YMCA Centre)
SLIEVENABROCK
437
DRINNAHILLY
254
Craignag
Walk 10
SLIEVENAMADDY
Ice House
Glen River Path
Black Stairs
SHAN SLIEVE
Pot of Pulgarve
SLIEVE COMMEDAGH
765
Glen River
THOMAS'S MOUNTAIN
Eagle Rock
The Castles
The Mourne Wall
Lesser Carn
Great Carn
853 (Trig Pillar)
849 (Living Rock)
SLIEVE DONARD
CROSS
Annalong Buttress
Brandy Pad
Walk 12
Crannoge
Bog of

The final climb to Slieve Commedagh

Gorse

10

S From the car park, TL and head up the road briefly. Just after a house on the left, you will find the Trassey Track on the left, beside a farm gate and a stone stile. Follow this track until you reach another gate (10min). Go through the gate and continue up the track. Up ahead you will see Slieve Meelmore and, behind it, Slieve Bearnagh. Pass through another gate and keep ahead on the track.

1 Cross a stream to arrive at a junction: keep SH (the left fork). Shortly afterwards, TL at another fork. After a few minutes, the sandy track becomes very rocky. Keep SH to climb SE up the rocky slope towards the saddle known as the Hares' Gap. There are a number of faint paths and it does not matter which one you take as long as you work your way roughly SE towards the saddle. Take care on the rocks in the wet.

2 1:00: Climb over the MW using a stile to arrive at the **Hares' Gap (437m)**. At the large cairn, TL (NE) and climb steeply alongside the MW, to the right of a rocky outcrop. As you gain height, the full extent of the stunning ridge which you will traverse becomes apparent, with the turret near the summit of Slieve Commedagh standing proud up on the right. Follow the MW as it undulates along the ridge.

3 2:10: Arrive at the turret near the summit of Slieve Commedagh which can be used as a shelter in bad conditions. Cross over the MW using a stile located immediately before the turret and walk NE. After a few minutes, arrive at the summit cairn of **Slieve Commedagh (765m)**. From the cairn, follow a faint path N which soon runs close to the edge of some high cliffs, offering fantastic views of Newcastle and Slieve Donard. Pass a cairn and keep following the path.

4 2:25: Arrive at another cairn on the summit of **Shan Slieve** (which is marked on the OSNI map but not on the Harvey map). Here, TL and head NW down a gentle grassy slope. Soon, you will catch sight of a dry-stone wall down to the NW: it runs E to W and then makes a right-angle turn to the N. As you follow the slope downhill to the NW, it gets progressively steeper. Soon, the tops of some cliffs come into view ahead to the NW: do not attempt to climb down these as they are very steep. Instead, make your way down to the right of the cliffs to meet the dry-stone wall. TL and follow the wall to the W. Just before the right-angle turn in the wall, cross a gully and keep following the wall on the other side. Watch your footing when descending into the gully as it is very steep.

5 At the right-angle turn in the wall, TR and follow it downhill (N). The ground all the way along the wall is uneven and quite difficult underfoot. Towards the end of the wall, the grass gets very long. When the wall ends, continue alongside a fence which soon arrives at another dry-stone wall: TL and follow this wall to the W.

6 After a few hundred metres, arrive at a stile near an old farm cottage. Cross the stile and follow a stony track to the cottage. Pass to the right of the cottage, now on a grassy track.

7 After a few minutes reach the edge of **Tollymore Forest Park**. Go through a gate into the forest and keep SH (N) on a stony track. Shortly afterwards, TL at a junction onto another track. After 5min, TR at the next junction of tracks. After another 5min, keep SH (W) at another junction, ignoring the paths to the left and right. After another 5min, at another junction, TR and descend.

8 After another 5min, TL at a junction of tracks. Immediately afterwards, TL at a fork. After a while, cross a stone stile and continue on the path on the other side. Keep SH (SW) and eventually, arrive back at the car park on the right.

Rime covering the turret on Slieve Donard on a cold winter's day

The High Mournes Epic Circuit

11

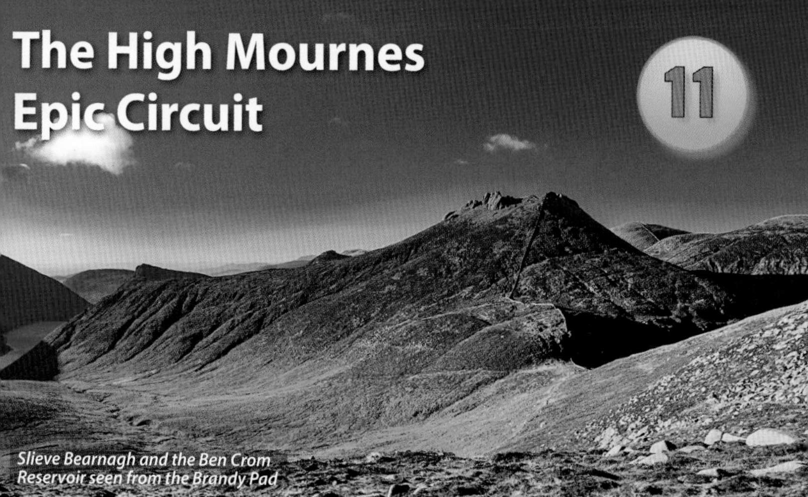

Slieve Bearnagh and the Ben Crom Reservoir seen from the Brandy Pad

If you could only do one walk in the Mourne Mountains, then this would probably be it. The route passes through some of the most spectacular scenery on the Island of Ireland. It starts with a traverse of the Brandy Pad, an old smugglers' path and one of the true highlights of these wonderful mountains. Then, it proceeds to climb the range's two highest peaks, Slieve Donard (849m) and Slieve Commedagh (765m). And finally, the return journey takes you along one of the best preserved and scenic sections of the MW. The views throughout are utterly exquisite. This is not a walk to be missed.

The route uses clear paths apart from two short sections: firstly, the final ascent to the Hares' Gap and secondly, the descent from the MW back to the Trassey Track. Both of these sections can be muddy and the paths are faint and intermittent. Navigation is relatively straightforward but, due to the high altitude, the walk should be saved for a fine day. Large sections of the route are along the MW which assists with route finding.

Time	5:45
Distance	16.7km 10.4miles
Ascent/Descent	1060m 3478ft
Maximum Altitude	849m 2786ft
Grade	Hard
Map	Map No. 4 (blue route)

Start/Finish: Trassey Track car park (158m; IG J 311314)

Access: From Newcastle, take the A50 NW towards Castlewellan. After just under 2 miles, TL onto the Ballyhafry Road towards Bryansford. After 2 miles, TL onto the Trassey Road and drive ¾mile to the car park on the left.

S From the car park, TL and head up the road briefly. Just after a house on the left, you will find the Trassey Track on the left (beside a farm gate and a stone stile). Follow this track until you reach another gate (10min). Go through the gate and continue up the track. Up ahead you will see Slieve Meelmore and, behind it, Slieve Bearnagh. Pass through another gate and keep ahead on the track.

1 Cross a stream to arrive at a junction: keep SH (the left fork). Shortly afterwards, TL at another fork. After a few minutes, the sandy track becomes very rocky. Keep SH to climb SE up the rocky slope towards the saddle known as the Hares' Gap. There are a number of faint paths and it does not matter which one you take as long as you work your way roughly SE towards the saddle. Take care on the rocks in the wet.

2 1:00: Climb over the MW on a stile to arrive at the **Hares' Gap (437m)** where there is a large cairn. Head E and pick up the path which can be seen snaking around the hillside to the SE. This is the **Brandy Pad**, an old smugglers' route. It takes you on a wonderful traverse across heather slopes all the way to the foot of Slieve Donard which looms large up ahead. See Walk 12 for further information on the Brandy Pad.

3 1:50: Keep SH past two large cairns.

4 2:40 Cross a stile over the MW. Immediately afterwards, TL to leave the Brandy Pad and walk uphill alongside the MW. The slope gets steeper as you ascend.

5 3:10: Finally, the slope levels off and you arrive at the summit of **Slieve Donard (849m)**. This is the highest point in Northern Ireland and the views of the entire Mourne range are magnificent. On a very clear day, the Wicklow Mountains near Dublin can even be spotted to the S. Cross the stile over the MW and walk downhill (initially W) still alongside the MW.

6 Keep SH across a saddle, still following the MW, and head up the slopes of Slieve Commedagh. Climb steeply until you reach the turret near the summit. Just after the turret, cross the MW on a stile and walk NE for a few minutes.

7 4:15: Arrive at the summit cairn of **Slieve Commedagh (765m)**. Retrace your steps back to the stile, climb over it and TR. Proceed along the path to the W, still following the MW. The sight of the MW snaking ahead of you all the way to the summit of Slieve Bearnagh is one of the iconic images of the Mourne Mountains.

8 5:05: Cross a stile over the MW and head NW on a rocky path. This peters out after a few metres and then becomes a faint path which soon runs (NW) just to the right of a shallow grassy gully. Soon the path becomes more clearly defined again. Descend on this path until it passes left into the gully: here do not enter the gully but keep SH (NW) on a faint and muddy path to the right of it. You will see the Trassey Track far below. It is possible to descend through the gully but this route is more difficult. Soon, the path becomes very muddy in places. Keep heading NW and the path becomes grassy again.

9 Eventually, the grassy path arrives just in front of a small hillock. Ignore the path which leads SH up the hillock: instead TL and descend to pick up another faint path.

10 Follow the path down to the Trassey Track. Then, TR and retrace your steps back to the start.

The Brandy Pad Traverse

12

Slieve Donard and the Castles seen from the Brandy Pad

This route traverses the main Mourne range using the full length of the Brandy Pad, an old smugglers' path and one of the highlights of these wonderful mountains. The walk travels from W to E and the views are incredible.

The route uses clear paths and navigation is straightforward, except for two short sections: firstly, the final ascent to the Hares' Gap and secondly, the first part of the descent from the MW. Both of these sections can be muddy and the paths there are faint and sometimes non-existent.

Time	4:20
Distance	11.9km 7.4miles
Ascent/Descent	440m/570m 1444ft/1870ft
Maximum Altitude	556m 1824ft
Grade	Medium
Map	Maps No. 4 & 1 (green route)

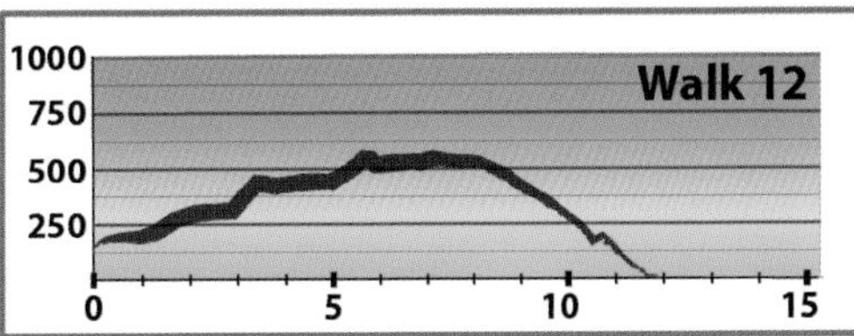

Start: Trassey Track car park (158m; IG J 311314)

Finish: Bloody Bridge car park (30m; IG J 389271)

Access: From Newcastle, take the A50 NW towards Castlewellan. After just under 2 miles, TL onto the Ballyhafry Road towards Bryansford. After 2 miles, TL onto Trassey Road and drive ¾mile to the Trassey car park on the left. Park a second car at the finish (see Walk 2 for directions) or use the Mourne Rambler bus service.

12

The Brandy Pad offers some of the finest views of Slieve Bearnagh

The Brandy Pad

Its proximity to the Isle of Man made Mourne country a haven for smugglers. During the 18th century, taxes in the Isle of Man were so low that smuggling goods to the shores of Britain and Ireland was profitable. Typically, the goods smuggled would be wine, spirits and tobacco but they also included tea, coffee, spices, sugar and any other goods that attracted high duties on mainland Britain or Ireland.

Smuggling was carried out predominantly by landing small boats on open beaches. From there, the goods would be placed in hiding holes or carried into the hills using smugglers' routes such as the Brandy Pad, which runs from the Bog of Donard, near the coast, to the Trassey Track further W. Goods would have been brought up to the Brandy Pad, from coastal landing spots, on various tracks leading to the head of the Annalong Valley including the Bloody Bridge River track. From there, they would have been carried W along the Brandy Pad to the Hares' Gap, down the Trassey Track and then to Hilltown for wider distribution.

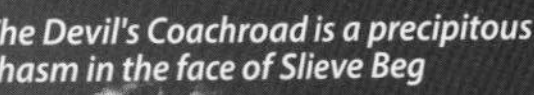

The Devil's Coachroad is a precipitous chasm in the face of Slieve Beg

12

S See Map 4. From the car park, TL and head up the road briefly. Just after a house, pick up the Trassey Track on the left (beside a farm gate and a stone stile). After 10min, go through another gate and continue SH. Slieve Meelmore and Slieve Bearnagh are now visible. Pass through another gate and keep SH on the track.

1 Cross a stream to arrive at a junction. Keep SH (the left fork). Shortly afterwards, TL at another fork. After a few minutes, the sandy track becomes rocky. Keep SH to climb SE up the slope towards a saddle up ahead. There are a number of faint paths here and it does not matter which one you take as long as you keep climbing roughly SE towards the saddle. The rocks are slippery in the wet.

2 1:00: Climb over the MW on a stile to arrive at the **Hares' Gap (437m)** where there is a large cairn. Head E and pick up a path which can be seen snaking to the SE: this is the **Brandy Pad** which makes a wonderful traverse across heather slopes all the way to the foot of Slieve Donard.

3 1:50: Keep SH past two large cairns.

4 2:40: Eventually, the Brandy Pad arrives at the MW (now see Map 1). Cross a stile and continue SH (E) on a path. This section is rocky and difficult and the path can be unclear: if in doubt, keep heading E close to the base of the valley.

5 Arrive at an old quarry. Look carefully for rocks in which there are man-made grooves. These were used by the masons to split the rocks. The path skirts around to the left of the quarry. After the quarry, continue down to the E on a clear track.

6 TL at junction and pick up a path. Shortly afterwards, cross a stile and descend some stone steps to a track. TL and walk along the track. Ford a river on some large boulders and immediately afterwards, go SH, briefly uphill: do not descend to the right. Follow the path all the way down to a road: cross it to arrive at the Bloody Bridge car park.

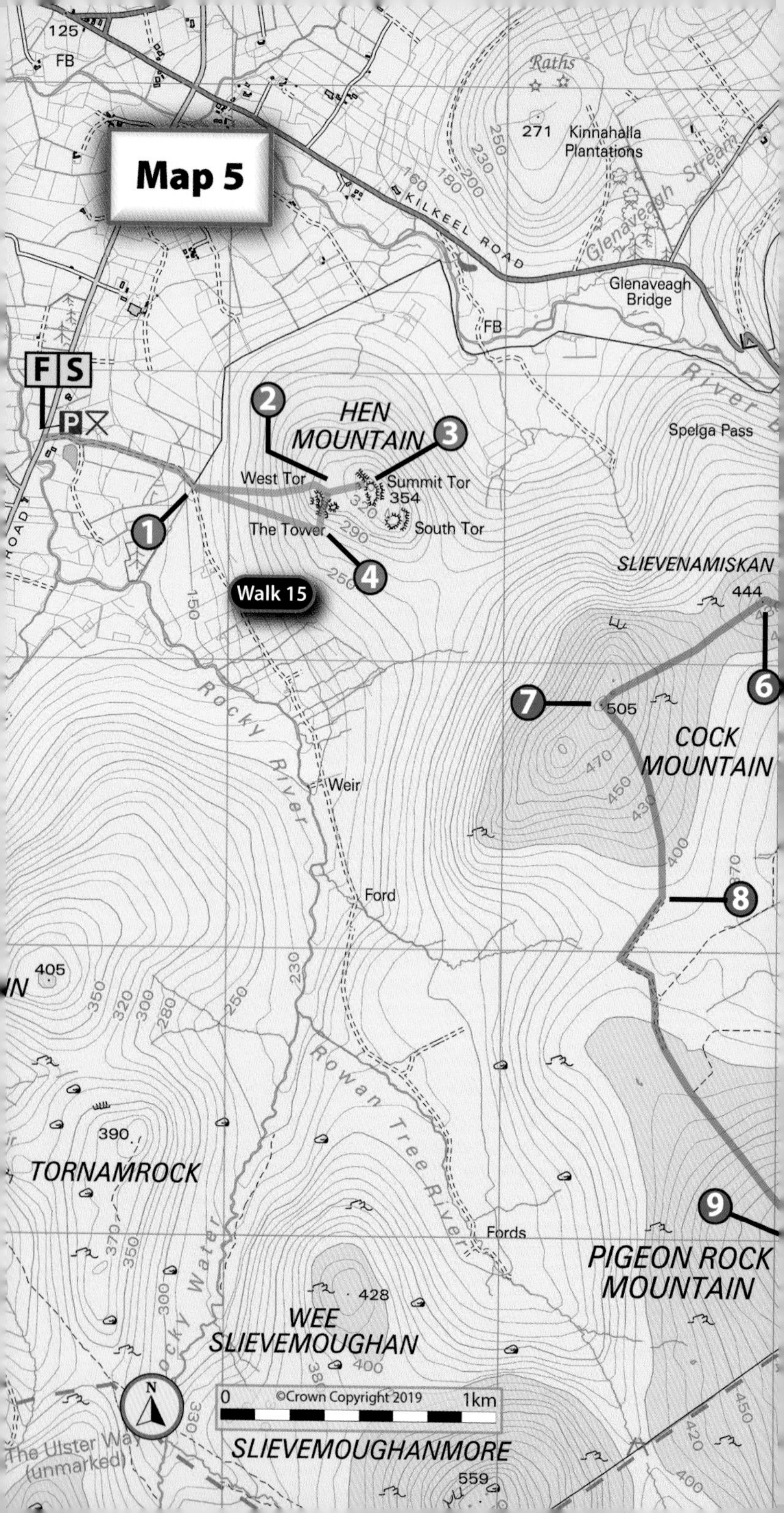

Map 5
125
FB
Raths
271
Kinnahalla Plantations
Glenaveagh Stream
KILKEEL ROAD
Glenaveagh Bridge
FB
River
Spelga Pass
F
S
P
HEN MOUNTAIN
West Tor
Summit Tor
354
South Tor
The Tower
Walk 15
SLIEVENAMISKAN
444
505
COCK MOUNTAIN
Rocky River
Weir
Ford
405
TORNAMROCK
390
Rowan Tree River
Fords
PIGEON ROCK MOUNTAIN
Rocky Water
428
WEE SLIEVEMOUGHAN
©Crown Copyright 2019
0
1km
N
The Ulster Way (unmarked)
SLIEVEMOUGHANMORE
559

SPALTHA
BUTTER MOUNTAIN
PELGA
Walk 13
Walk 14
SLIEVENAMAN ROAD
Fofanny Dam (Reservoir)
Pass
FB
Weir
SLIEVENAMUCK
The Ulster Way
OTT MOUNTAIN
Spelga Dam (Reservoir)
Deers Meadow
River Bann
Drumlea Stream
Source of River Bann
Sheep pen
CARN MOUNTAIN
SLIEVE MUCK
Miners Hole River
White Water
479
472
490
315
557
588
674
534
626

13

Hen Mountain viewed from the summit of Cock Mountain

The Gravity Defying Lane!

This lane is quite famous for its apparent ability to defy gravity. If you park your car at the gate, leave it in neutral and then release the brake, the car will roll 'up' the hill towards the main road. Sadly, this is not the result of magic but is an optical illusion: the car is of course running downhill although the terrain makes it look as if it is going uphill. Try it. It is pretty cool.

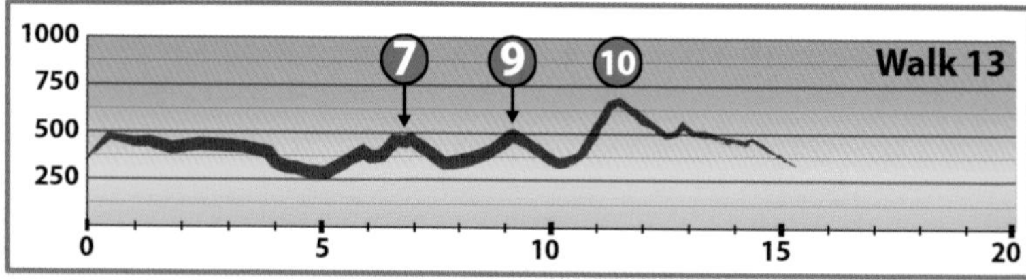

Tour of Spelga Dam

13

Walk 13 makes a complete circuit of Spelga Dam

On a fine day, this challenging walk will be one of the highlights of a trip to the Mournes. The route takes the adventurous walker away from the more frequented hotspots (such as Slieve Donard) and crosses little-trodden ground on its way over no less than nine named peaks: Slievenamuck (504m), Butter Mountain (492m), Spelga (472m), Slievenamiskan (444m), Cock Mountain (505m), Pigeon Rock (534m), Slieve Muck (674m), Carn (588m) and Ott (524m). The vistas throughout are spectacular.

The route, however, does not give up its attractions easily. It is almost entirely across heathery terrain which is often wet underfoot. Make sure that you do not forget your gaiters! Often there are no paths so careful navigation is required. On the section between Cock Mountain and Pigeon Rock, there is a fine line between picking the correct route with firm ground and the wrong wet one.

Time	6:00
Distance	15.4km 9.6miles
Ascent/Descent	1050m 3445ft
Maximum Altitude	674m 2211ft
Grade	Very hard
Map	Map No. 5 (blue route)

Start/Finish: Ott Mountain car park (379m; IG J 280278)

Access: From Newcastle, take the A50 NW towards Castlewellan. After just under 2 miles, TL onto the Ballyhafry Road (B180) towards Bryansford. Pass through Bryansford and then after 2¼ miles, TL at a junction ('Silent Valley'). After 3½ miles arrive at the car park on the right.

S From the W side of the car park, take a path of stone blocks initially NW. After a few metres, the path bends to the left, becoming grassy and then climbs over a stile. Now climb the grassy slope (NW) on a faint path, following a waymark for the Ulster Way: ignore other paths on the right.

1 0:15: Just before the top of the slope, TL onto another path and climb the last few metres to the summit of **Slievenamuck (504m)**. The views of the Slieve Meelmore ridge and Spelga Reservoir are fantastic. From the summit, retrace your steps for a few metres and, when you meet the path of your ascent, keep SH (NE) along a faint grassy path. Ignore paths to the left and right and keep heading NE until you arrive at a sheep fence (5-10min from Slievenamuck). Climb over the fence and continue SH on a faint path running NNE alongside, and to the left of, another fence. Ignore waymarks for the Mourne Way heading to the left.

2 0:35: Arrive at the indistinct **Butter Mountain (492m)** where there is little to indicate that you are at the summit. Continue N alongside the fence for a few minutes. Descend briefly and then, before a small rise, TL (W) on a faint grassy path which makes its way towards a fence far off to the W. The path soon bends to the NW. If you cannot locate the path then just head NW towards the right side of the fence. Ensure that you do not descend to the N. Just before the fence, TL (SW) onto a faint track and climb briefly.

3 Arrive at a post (with waymarks on it) beside the fence. Climb the fence and proceed W on a faint path. Soon, the path bends to the SW and continues close to the top of the ridgeline. 1hr from the start, TL at a faint junction of paths: if you cannot locate this junction, simply continue SW, keeping near the top of the ridge.

4 1:10: From the summit cairn of **Spelga Mountain (472m)**, proceed SE across the grassy slopes, descending towards Spelga Reservoir. Ensure that you do not stray too far to the right (S) where the slope gets much steeper and there are rocky outcrops. When the car park at Spelga Reservoir comes into view, head towards the left (E) side of it. Just before arriving at the main road, ford a stream on some rocks. Be careful as the rocks can be slippery.

5 Immediately afterwards, go through a gate and cross the road. TR and walk W through the car park. At the end of the car park, walk down the road for a few minutes. About 100m after a house on the left, TL along a tarmac lane (see information box on page 70) and arrive at a metal gate. Climb the metal gate and continue towards Spelga Dam. Note that, although this is a popular route, it is not clear whether walkers are actually permitted here. Just in front of the dam, pass through a gate and cross a bridge over the dam run-off canals. Then, proceed on a faint grassy path uphill with the dam towering above you on the left. Soon, rise above the dam: continue SW on the path. After a few minutes, at a rock, the path turns right and heads briefly NW towards a fence. Cross the fence and continue on a path heading initially W up the slope. When the path all but disappears, keep heading straight uphill towards the summit.

6 2:10: Arrive at the summit of **Slievenamiskan (444m)**. Continue SW on a faint path and descend to a saddle below Cock Mountain. Then, continue SW on the faint path up the other side of the saddle. When the path disappears, continue to work your way broadly SW up the heathery slope towards the summit.

7 2:40: From the north summit of **Cock Mountain (505m)**, continue SW on a path to descend to a small saddle. Then climb to the south summit. Now head briefly E to descend some rocks. Then, head SE across uneven heathery ground towards the left tip of an old raised bog road which is shaped like an 'L'. Keep to the high ground for as long as you can (the low ground is more boggy). A few hundred metres before the bog road, you should pick up a path which takes you to it. If you cannot locate the path, then simply proceed across the heather to the bog road.

Slieve Muck seen from the summit of Pigeon Rock Mountain

13

8 TR onto the bog road. After a few minutes, it makes a right-angle turn to the left and continues SE. After a few more minutes, the bog road bends to the right and climbs gently uphill to the S. When the bog road peters out at a grassy plateau, TL and proceed SSE up a grassy slope which gradually increases in gradient. You may find a path from the plateau to the summit of Pigeon Rock but it is patchy. Eventually, when a stile comes into view, make for it.

9 3:45: Arrive at the stile and cairn at the summit of **Pigeon Rock Mountain (534m)**. Follow a dry-stone wall NE downhill: stay on the left side (N) of the wall. Eventually, cross a stile near a road (B27) and head E towards another stile. Cross the B27 and then cross the stile. Then head uphill (E) alongside a wall.

10 4:45: After a very steep climb, arrive at the trig point on the summit of **Slieve Muck (674m)**. If you have climbed this peak in autumn, then you will know that it is aptly named. Just to the NE of the summit are two stiles. Climb over the left one and walk alongside the MW, heading N. After 20-25min, when the MW bends to the right, keep following it E.

11 5:20: Climb to the summit of **Carn Mountain (588m)**. Then, keep following the MW as it descends (N). Soon the wall climbs again briefly and, at the top of a rise (557m), a stile comes into view to the NNE. At this point, TL and head NW, descending gently away from the MW, across uneven slopes of peat and grass towards Ott Mountain. Do not start to head towards Ott before this point as the peat hags are more challenging to the S. The gradient levels out and then starts climbing again up the slopes of Ott: keep heading NW.

12 5:40: From the summit of **Ott Mountain (524m)**, follow a faint path NW along the crest of the wide ridge. When the path disappears, keep heading along the crest (NW and then N) towards the car park which can be seen ahead. Finally, when the ridge descends to a track, TL. After a few minutes, climb a stile and cross the road to arrive back at the start.

S From the car park, head briefly E up the road to a gate by a stream. Go through the gate and proceed upwards on a wide track to the NE. After a few minutes, at a corrugated iron livestock pen, leave the main track in favour of a broad grassy path on the right heading NE up the slope.

1 0:25: Arrive at the summit of **Slievenamuck (504m)** with fantastic views of the Slieve Meelmore ridge and Spelga Reservoir. Walk NE and shortly afterwards, keep SH along a faint grassy path. Ignore paths to the left and right and keep heading NE until you arrive at a sheep fence (10min from Slievenamuck). Climb over the fence and continue SH on a faint path running NNE alongside, and to the left of, another fence. Ignore 'Mourne Way' waymarks heading to the left.

2 0:55: Arrive at the broad, indistinct **Butter Mountain (492m)**. There is little to indicate the summit save that it is the high point. From the summit, continue N alongside the fence for a few minutes. Descend briefly and then, before a small rise, TL (W) on a faint grassy path which makes its way towards a fence far off to the W. The path soon bends to the NW. If you cannot locate the path then just head NW towards the right side of the fence. Ensure that you do not descend to the N. Just before the fence, TL (SW) onto another faint path and climb briefly.

3 Arrive at a post (with waymarks) beside the fence. Climb the fence and proceed W on a faint path. Soon, the path bends to the SW and continues close to the top of the ridge. TL at a faint junction of paths: if you cannot locate this junction, simply continue SW, keeping near the crest of the ridge.

4 1:40: From the summit cairn on **Spelga Mountain (472m)**, proceed SE across the grassy slopes, descending towards Spelga Reservoir. Ensure that you do not stray too far to the right (S) where the slope is steeper and there are crags. When the car park comes into view, head towards the left (E) side of it. Just before the road, ford a stream on some rocks: the rocks can be slippery. Immediately afterwards, go through the gate passed earlier, cross the road and enter the car park.

Butter Mountain Horseshoe

14

The Butter Mountain ridge overlooks Spelga Reservoir

This little-used route is spectacular. A short easy climb takes you onto a lovely ridge where you remain for the duration. The views of the high Mournes and Spelga Dam are magnificent. The ground can be wet underfoot and navigation after Butter Mountain is slightly tricky because the path is intermittent.

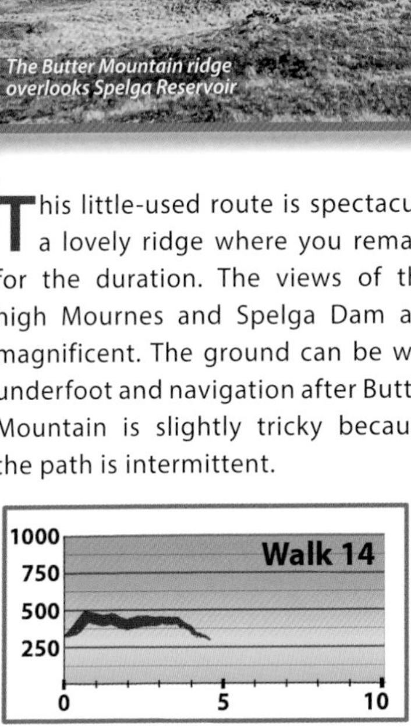

Time	2:00
Distance	4.8km 3.0miles
Ascent/Descent	210m 689ft
Maximum Altitude	504m 1654ft
Grade	Easy
Map	Map No. 5 (red route)

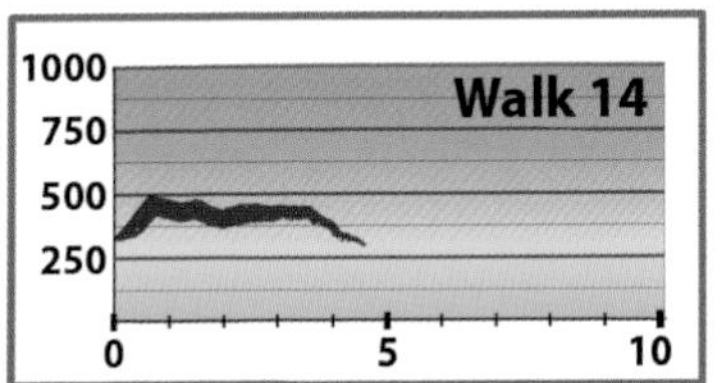

Start/Finish: Spelga Dam car park (345m; IG J 268273)

Access: From Newcastle, take the A50 NW towards Castlewellan. After just under 2 miles, TL onto the Ballyhafry Road (B180) towards Bryansford. Pass through Bryansford and then after 2¼ miles, TL at a junction ('Silent Valley'). After 4 miles, TR onto the B27. After ½mile, arrive at the car park on the left.

The track leading to Hen Mountain

S From the car park, cross the road and walk E along a track.

1 0:10: Go through a gate and TL to climb E up the grassy slope towards the W tor of Hen Mountain. There is a well-trodden grassy path which eventually passes to the left of the summit outcrops. Here you should pass an old millstone: in fact, there are many millstones on the slopes of Hen Mountain in various stages of construction. On arrival at a grassy spur, the faint path bends to the right and works its way up between rocks.

2 After a few minutes arrive in front of the W tor. Start the final climb from the left (E) of the tor and climb diagonally across grass onto granite. Then, climb straight upwards. From the **W tor of Hen Mountain (337m)**, the views are magnificent. Descend again and proceed E.

3 Climb to arrive at the **middle tor of Hen Mountain (361m)** which is the highest point on the mountain. Retrace your steps back to the base of the W tor. Pass down through a cleft between the rocks of the W tor and then descend SW on a grassy path.

4 Shortly afterwards, TR onto another path descending across the slopes towards the gate passed earlier (Waypoint no. 1). Go through the gate and retrace your steps to the car park.

Hen Mountain

15

The wonderful summit tors of Hen Mountain

Hen Mountain is popular with families because it is a short, straightforward climb offering superb views. The exposure on the rocky tors is thrilling. It is a great mountain for parents seeking to introduce their children to the delights of hill walking. Navigation is straightforward. Take care at the summits as the drops are sheer.

Time	1:15
Distance	3.0km 1.9miles
Ascent/Descent	230m 755ft
Maximum Altitude	361m 1184ft
Grade	Easy
Map	Map No. 5 (green route)

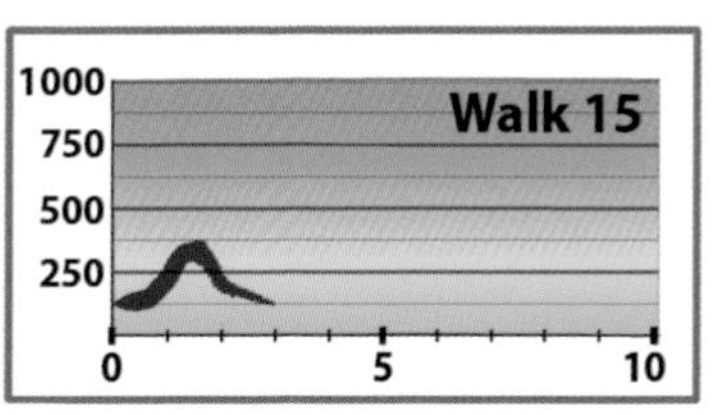

Start/Finish: Sandbank Road car park (130m; IG J 233277)

Access: From the centre of Hilltown, head E on the B27 ('Newry'). After ½mile, TR ('Silent Valley') and continue on the B27. After 1 mile, TR onto a minor road ('Santa's Cottage' and 'Rostrevor'). After ¾mile, arrive at the car park on the right.

The cairn on the summit of Eagle Mountain

Map 6
HEN MOUNTAIN
Walk 16
West Tor
Summit Tor
354
The Tower
South Tor
Spelga Pass
River Bann
B27
FB
SLIEVENAMISKAN
444
COCK MOUNTAIN
505
Rocky River
Weir
Ford
405
Walk 18
Rowan Tree River
Fords
390
TORNAMROCK
PIGEON ROCK MOUNTAIN
534
428
WEE SLIEVEMOUGHAN
Rocky Water
SLIEVEMOUGHANMORE
559
The Ulster Way (unmarked)
Pierces Castle
Windy Gap
Pigeon Rock River
EAGLE MOUNTAIN
638
The Slates
Ford
The Forks
Shanlough
626
SHANLIEVE
Great Gully
Ford
Pigeon Ro
Left H Buttr
0
1km
©Crown Copyright 2019

Batt's Wall runs close to the summit of Slievemoughanmore

Western Mournes Nine Peak Circuit

16

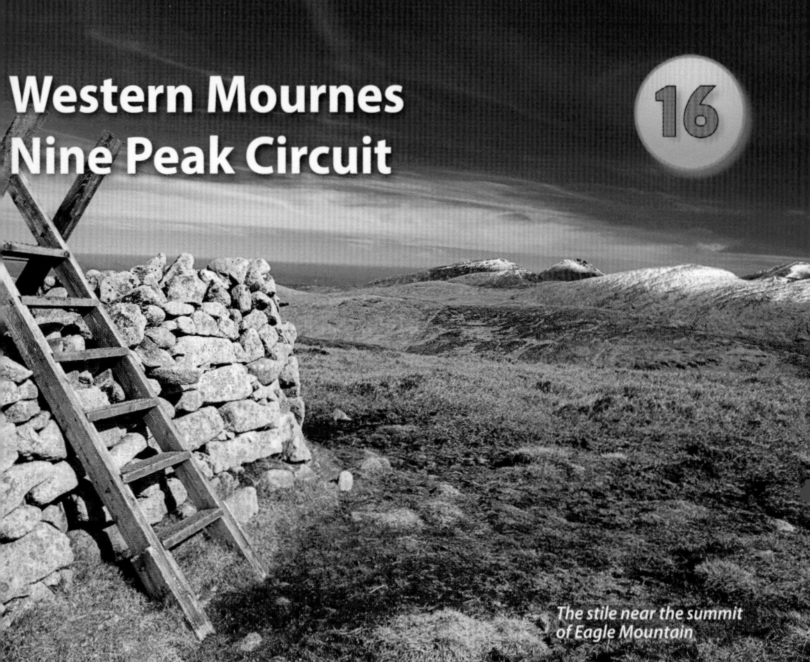

The stile near the summit of Eagle Mountain

This epic circuit climbs nine summits of the Western Mournes and is one of the finest walks in the region. Views are spectacular throughout but perhaps the highlight is the rarely climbed summit of Eagle Mountain which overlooks the entire range. The hills around the first third of the route were apparently used in Game of Thrones as the landscape for Bran Stark's flight north of Winterfell.

The route is tough with many steep climbs and descents. The terrain and navigation are challenging as there are long sections without paths, sometimes across wet, boggy ground. Accordingly, this is not a walk for beginners. This route would be most enjoyable in late spring, summer or early autumn when the ground is drier.

Time	7:00
Distance	17.1km 10.6miles
Ascent/Descent	1255m 4118ft
Maximum Altitude	638m 2093ft
Grade	Very hard
Map	Map No. 6 (red route)

Start/Finish: Sandbank Road car park (130m; IG J 233277)

Access: From the centre of Hilltown, head E on the B27 ('Newry'). After ½mile, TR ('Silent Valley') and continue on the B27. After 1 mile, TR onto a minor road ('Santa's Cottage' and 'Rostrevor'). After ¾mile, arrive at the car park on the right.

S From the car park, cross the road and walk E along a track. After 5-10min, go through a gate and continue S along a track. After 5min, TR at a wooden post, heading SW down a grassy slope directly towards Rocky Mountain: there is no path. At Rocky River, walk along the bank to find a safe place to cross: the banks are shallower directly below the summit of Rocky Mountain. Ford the river on boulders which can be slippery. Then, climb straight up grassy slopes towards the summit of Rocky Mountain: again there is no path and the going is tough.

1 1:00: At the summit of **Rocky Mountain (405m)**, TL (S) to pick up a grassy path heading down towards a saddle. Head straight across the saddle on a faint path and climb towards some rocky outcrops.

2 1:20: Pass through the outcrops to arrive at the summit of **Tornamrock (390m)**. Head along the ridge directly towards the pointy peak of Pierce's Castle. There is a short section of peat hags to be negotiated. Eventually, the path descends to a saddle and continues up the other side. If the path disappears, then just keep heading upwards towards the left of the summit outcrops.

3 2:00: Skirt around the left of the first outcrop and then climb up through the rocks to the summit of **Pierce's Castle (467m)**. Before the summit, scramble up a steep rock step. Descend SW towards a clear path. Shortly after the route levels off, ignore a track on the left heading SE. Shortly, TL on a track heading S. After a few minutes, at a crossroad, TL onto a faint path. At another junction, TL and continue SW. About 100m before a fence, leave the track (which soon disappears) and proceed SSE towards the fence: try to keep to the firm ground.

4 At the fence, TL and walk alongside it. This section is boggy so gaiters are useful. When the fence arrives at a dry-stone wall, climb alongside it. The gradient increases as you climb and the final section is very steep.

5 3:00: At the summit cairn of **Shanlieve (626m)**, the wall bends to the left: follow it NE, descending to a saddle and then climbing up the other side to a stile. Cross the stile and walk briefly SE to the summit cairn of **Eagle Mountain (638m; 3hr15min)**. The views here are amongst the finest in the whole range with Slieve Binnian, Slieve Bearnagh and Slieve Donard all visible. Retrace your steps back to the wall and TR to follow it NW. When the wall bends to the right, continue to follow it downwards, steeply in places.

6 3:45: Arrive at a saddle, the **Windy Gap (407m)** where there are two stiles: cross the left one. Then, TR and climb NE alongside the wall. After 15-20min of steep climbing, when the gradient levels, TL (N) and climb to a cairn on top of a rock.

7 4:15: From the cairn, head to another large cairn to the NE: this marks the summit of **Slievemoughanmore (559m)** which offers splendid views of Spelga Dam and the Western Mournes. Head SE and descend to arrive back at the wall again. Then, descend the steep and slippery slope alongside the wall. At a saddle, keep SH and climb NE, still alongside the wall. Follow the wall when it bends to the left.

8 5:00: After a few more minutes, arrive at the summit cairn of **Pigeon Rock Mountain (534m)**. Head NW down a grassy slope to a plateau: you should find a faint path. Aim to arrive at the middle of the plateau, picking up a path which divides the boggy ground to the right from the firm heathery ground to the left: the difference between the two terrain types is clearly discernible. Make sure that you do not drop too far to the right into the bog. Head NW across the plateau until the path disappears into heather. Then, TR briefly towards Spelga Reservoir to locate an old bog road: follow that initially N. After a few minutes, the bog road bends to the right and arrives at a junction: TL, heading NW on a grassy track. After another few minutes, when the track splits, TR onto a faint grassy path heading N. When the path vanishes, continue N. Shortly afterwards, TR onto a path and climb, initially NE. Soon the path bends to the N and climbs

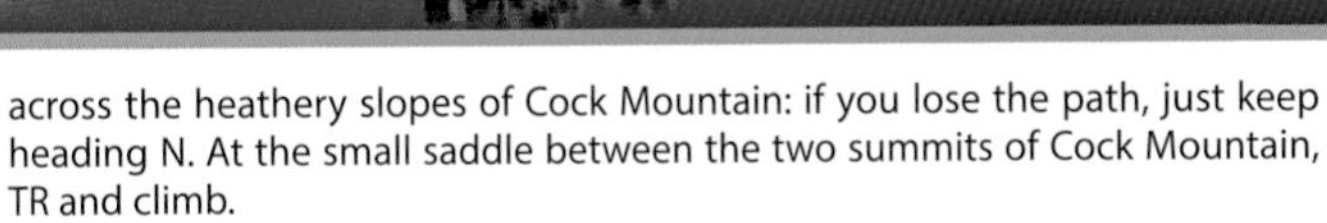

Reflections of Batt's Wall. Slieve Muck is the peak in the background

across the heathery slopes of Cock Mountain: if you lose the path, just keep heading N. At the small saddle between the two summits of Cock Mountain, TR and climb.

9 6:00: Arrive on the N summit of **Cock Mountain (505m)**. From the summit cairn, head W and pick up a faint path. The path soon bends to the right and descends (NW) on a very steep, heathery slope. It then crosses a saddle and climbs the slopes of Hen Mountain. Next, the path skirts around to the N side of Hen Mountain and climbs to a small saddle between rocky summits: TL and climb SE.

10 6:30: After a few minutes arrive at the **S tor of Hen Mountain (354m)**. Return to the saddle and go SH to climb the **middle tor (361m)**: you will need to scramble up some rocks. Alternatively, TL at the saddle to skirt around the base of the middle tor towards the W tor. From the middle tor, head W to find a path running down to the NW. Near the foot of the slope, TL and walk to the **W tor (337m)**. Pass down through a cleft between the rocks of the W tor and then descend SW on a grassy path. Shortly afterwards, TR onto another path, descending W across the slopes. Go through the gate passed earlier and retrace your steps to the car park.

The hills near Leitrim Lodge were apparently used in Game of Thrones

Mass Rocks

In the 17th and 18th centuries, penal laws were passed in Ireland to attempt to force Irish Roman Catholics and Protestant dissenters (such as Presbyterians) to accept the reformed denomination of the Anglican Church which was practised by the state established Church of Ireland. Accordingly, holding and attending Catholic and Presbyterian services was a perilous affair. Bishops were banished and priests had to register to preach. Unbelievably, priest hunters were employed to arrest unregistered priests and Presbyterian preachers.

Isolated locations were therefore sought to hold religious ceremonies and frequently mass rocks were used. Often a stone would be taken from a church ruin and moved to a remote rural area: a cross would be carved on top. Because the activity was illegal, the services were not scheduled and their occurrence was communicated by word of mouth. The practice had waned by the late 17th century, when many services moved to thatched mass houses.

Pierce's Castle & the Rocky Ridge

17

The rocky summit of Pierce's Castle

Pierce's Castle is a popular peak but most people take the direct route up the broad track from Leitrim Lodge and then return the same way. The route described here, however, takes you on a beautiful circuit of little used paths and travels the stunning ridge between Pierce's Castle and Rocky Mountain. The nearby hills were apparently used in Game of Thrones as the landscape for Bran Stark's flight north of Winterfell. It is not a difficult route and route finding should be straightforward. Watch out for mountain bikers on the SW section of the route.

Time	3:40
Distance	11.5km 7.1miles
Ascent/Descent	530m 1739ft
Maximum Altitude	467m 1532ft
Grade	Medium
Map	Map No. 6 (blue route)

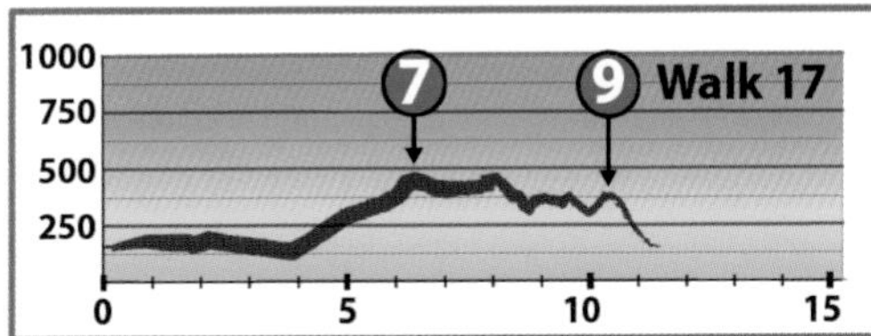

Start/Finish: Leitrim Lodge car park (173m; IG J 224256)

Access: From the centre of Hilltown, head E on the B27 ('Newry'). After about ½mile, TR ('Silent Valley') and continue on the B27. After 1 mile, TR onto a small road ('Santa's Cottage' and 'Rostrevor'). After 2¼ miles, arrive at Leitrim Lodge car park on the left.

17

S From the information board to the S of the car park, take a path running SE. Shortly, go through a gate and cross a bridge to continue along a track heading SE. After a few minutes, when the main track bends left, TR onto a path, initially heading S. The path soon fords a stream and then continues SW. Follow the frequent waymarks for the 'Mourne Way'.

1 0:25: When the path arrives at a pine forest, there is an old mass rock on the left (with an altar and cross carved on the top). Immediately after the mass rock, keep SH along the left side of the forest ('Mourne Way' waymarks). After a few minutes, ford another stream and continue on the path (SW). Cross a stile and continue SW on a track ('Mourne Way').

2 0:45: Keep on the track until you meet another track: TL ('Mourne Way'). This track heads uphill and then bends to the left away from the Yellow Water River: do not cross the bridge on the right. Take care here as you will be crossing mountain bike tracks. After about 10min of climbing, at a junction of tracks, follow the main track around to the right and continue uphill. After another 10min, at another junction of tracks, keep SH (E). Again, be careful as this is a crossing point for mountain bikes.

3 After a few more minutes, leave the track in favour of a grassy path on the left. This junction is easy to miss: if you reach a bridge on the track then you have gone slightly too far. The grassy path proceeds N up through a clearing between trees. Soon, the path becomes faint and the trees close in. At a fork of faint paths, TL, crossing a small footbridge and heading into the trees. The path between the trees initially heads uphill (N) but soon bends to the right (NE).

4 Arrive at a low sheep fence: there used to be a stile here but it has disappeared. Climb over the fence and continue on a muddy path heading uphill to the NE. The peaks to your right are Eagle Mountain and Shanlieve. When the path arrives at a dry-stone wall, TL and walk alongside it (W) for a few metres. Just where the wall peters out, climb over a low sheep fence. Continue initially NE on a faint muddy path which heads across a peat bog.

5 Soon the path bends around to the E and arrives at a junction of tracks. TL and proceed along an old raised bog road. Up ahead, you will see the small, boulder strewn, peak of Pierce's Castle.

6 When the bog road reaches a track, TR and head initially SE. Soon the track bends around to the left and makes its way N directly towards Pierce's Castle. Ignore any offshoots on the right.

7 2:20: Finally, the path climbs up through boulders to arrive on the summit of **Pierce's Castle (467m)**. Proceed to the left of the enormous boulder on the summit and pick up a path heading down to the N. Shortly afterwards, there is a steep rock step and it may be advisable to descend (rather unflatteringly) on your backside. Just after the rock step, the path descends to the NE, slightly to the right of the ridge. But soon the path arrives on top of the broad ridge again: keep heading N. The path becomes faint in places: keep near the crest of the ridge. When the path descends to a small saddle, keep SH (N) and head up the slope on the other side of the saddle to arrive on a long, broad plateau.

8 3:00: Keep N along the plateau to arrive on the summit of **Tornamrock (390m)**. Keep to the left of the rocky outcrops and descend directly towards Rocky Mountain (NW): the path is faint in places. After 5min, arrive at a saddle between Tornamrock and Rocky Mountain: continue on a faint path up the slope of Rocky Mountain on the other side of the saddle.

9 3:15: After 10min arrive at the summit cairn of **Rocky Mountain (405m)**. From here, Carlingford Lough and the town of Rostrevor can be seen to the SW. Head W across the summit on a faint path. Soon, the path begins to descend steeply to the SW towards a track that can be seen below. Work your way down the steep slope to the track. TR and follow the track back to the car park.

Slievemoughanmore & Rocky River Valley

18

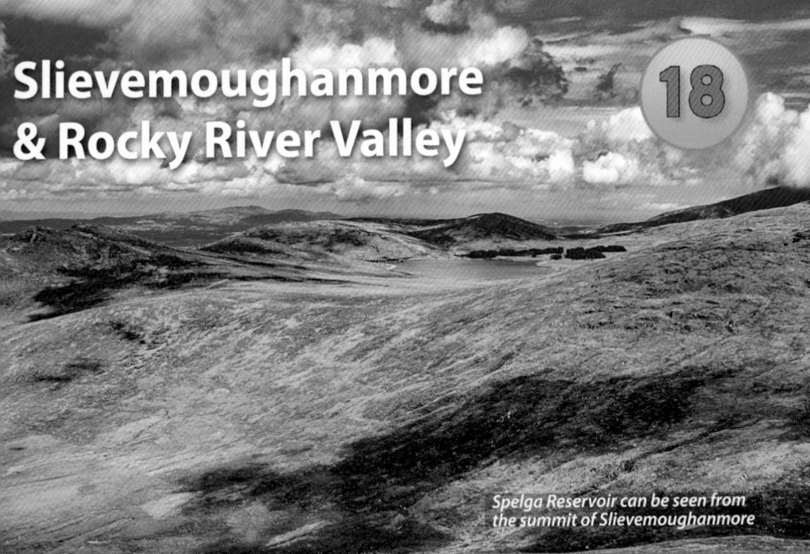

Spelga Reservoir can be seen from the summit of Slievemoughanmore

This is a little known and challenging route up Slievemoughanmore, one of the more inaccessible peaks in the Mournes. From the summit, the wide-ranging views are magnificent and you will be able to enjoy them in peace and quiet as the isolated location seems to deter all but the hardiest walkers. The nearby hills were apparently used in Game of Thrones as the landscape for Bran Stark's flight north of Winterfell.

Time	4:00
Distance	10.2km 6.3miles
Ascent/Descent	640m 2100ft
Maximum Altitude	559m 1834ft
Grade	Hard
Map	Map No. 6 (green route)

Much of the route is across boggy and uneven ground without paths. Navigation is tricky between Pierce's Castle and the Windy Gap. And the final climb of Slievemoughanmore is steep and slippery in the wet, as is the initial part of the descent. The junction before crossing the Rowan Tree River is hard to locate.

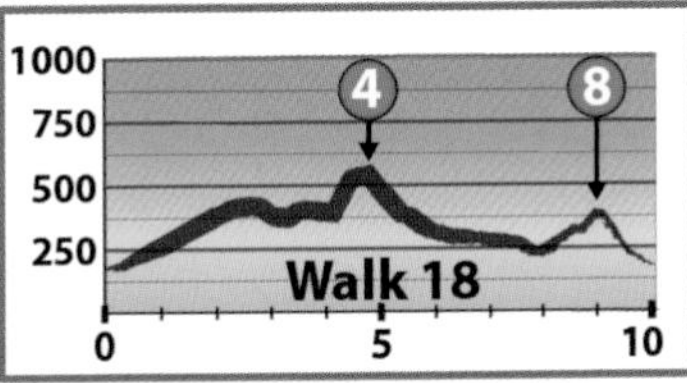

Start/Finish: Leitrim Lodge car park (173m; IG J 224256)

Access: From the centre of Hilltown, head E on the B27 ('Newry'). After about ½mile, TR ('Silent Valley') and continue on the B27. After 1 mile, TR onto a small road ('Santa's Cottage' and 'Rostrevor'). After 2¼ miles, arrive at Leitrim Lodge car park on the left.

S From the information boards to the S of the car park, take a paved path running SE. Shortly afterwards, go through a gate and then cross a bridge to continue along a stony track heading SE. After a few minutes, continue on the track as it bends to the left and begins to climb: ignore a grassy track branching off to the right. Soon, the track bears around to the right and continues climbing (S). The vibrant pink heather is beautiful in the summer months.

1 At a junction of paths with a large cairn in the middle, keep left (SE) to head in the direction of a long whale-back ridge: the two highest mountains on the ridge are Eagle Mountain and Shanlieve. Ignore a number of paths/tracks branching off to the right and keep on the main path. Eventually, the path bends around to the N and heads directly towards the nearby summit of Pierce's Castle: do not climb the peak but instead take a faint path on the right heading E. When the path disappears, continue to work your way down the slope in the direction of Slievemoughanmore, the flat-topped mountain to the E which has a dry-stone wall running up its flank. The ground is uneven so watch your footing.

2 Cross the river at the base of the slope. Then, climb the steep grassy slope of a spur on the other side, still heading E. This section is hard work. Crest the grassy spur and then, keeping your altitude, contour around it, eventually heading SE. Do not lose much altitude or you will have to gain it again later. When you see a small saddle to the SE (known as the Windy Gap), you should make for it.

3 1:30: TL at the wall at the **Windy Gap (407m)** and follow it upwards to the NE: stay to the left of the wall. After 15-20min of steep climbing, when the gradient eases, TL (N) and climb towards a cairn on top of a rock.

4 2:00: On arrival at the cairn, head for another large cairn a few metres away to the NE: this marks the summit of **Slievemoughanmore (559m)**. Head E and descend to arrive back at the wall again: descend alongside it. The descent is very steep and slippery in places.

5 At the base of the slope, cross the Rowan Tree River. Then, just after a stile, TL on a faint path running parallel to the river (NW). When the path disappears, follow the river (keeping on its right) across fairly boggy ground. When you meet a track, follow it NW.

6 After 15–20min on the track, leave it in favour of a very faint grassy track on the left **(coordinates IG J 246256)**: this junction is difficult to spot and if you are still on the main track when it heads N then you have gone past it. From the junction, head towards the Rowan Tree River and follow the right bank for a few minutes until you reach a crossing point where the river runs across a huge flat rock. If you were not able to locate the junction, then simply head to the Rowan Tree River and make your way upriver (SE) until you find a safe crossing point. After crossing the river, descend on the left bank where there is a faint grassy path: follow the path down to a footbridge and cross the Rocky Water. Once on the other side, go SH (W) up the grassy slope. The ground can be boggy after heavy rain. You will be aiming for the saddle above to the W. As you climb, angle towards a stream and gully on the right where you will find a few waymarks. Soon, the path crosses over the gully (near a post with a waymark) and continues up to the W on the other side.

7 3:25: Eventually, the path reaches the saddle below Rocky Mountain. Do not head to the W side of the saddle but instead TR (N) and take a faint path running straight up to the peak of Rocky Mountain: this path is easy to miss.

8 3:35: Arrive at the summit cairn of **Rocky Mountain (405m)**. From here, Carlingford Lough and the town of Rostrevor can be seen to the SW. Head W across the summit on a faint path. Soon, the path begins to descend steeply to the SW towards the track climbed at the start of the walk. Work your way down the steep slope to the track: TR and descend to the car park.

Doan & Carn Circuit

19

Doan overlooks the stunning Lough Shannagh

This amazing, yet quiet, circuit is right in the heart of the main Mourne range and is perhaps our favourite route. A straightforward track leads through a magnificent valley to the delightful Lough Shannagh. Here, the route leaves the beaten track to climb Doan: a little-known mountain which, due to its central position amongst the highest peaks in the range, offers maybe the finest viewpoint in the Mournes. The return journey takes you over Carn Mountain alongside a beautiful section of the MW.

Time	4:45
Distance	14.6km 9.1miles
Ascent/Descent	530m 1739ft
Maximum Altitude	594m 1949ft
Grade	Medium
Map	Map No. 7 (red route)

The route is not particularly challenging apart from a few short sections without paths over uneven ground: take care on these sections to avoid twisting an ankle and pay close attention to navigation too.

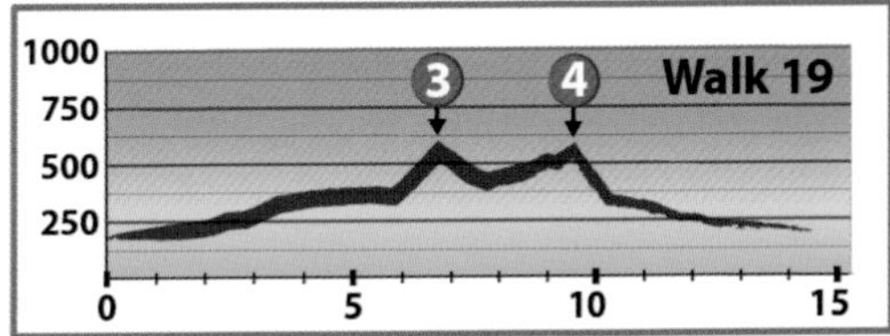

Start/Finish: Banns Road car park (194m; IG J 285214)

Access: From Newcastle, take the A50 NW towards Castlewellan. After just under 2 miles, TL onto the Ballyhafry Road (B180) towards Bryansford. Pass through Bryansford and then after 2¼ miles, TL at a junction ('Silent Valley'). Drive for 7.8 miles, passing Spelga Reservoir and Crocknafeola Forest, to arrive at a car park on the left beside a horse riding centre.

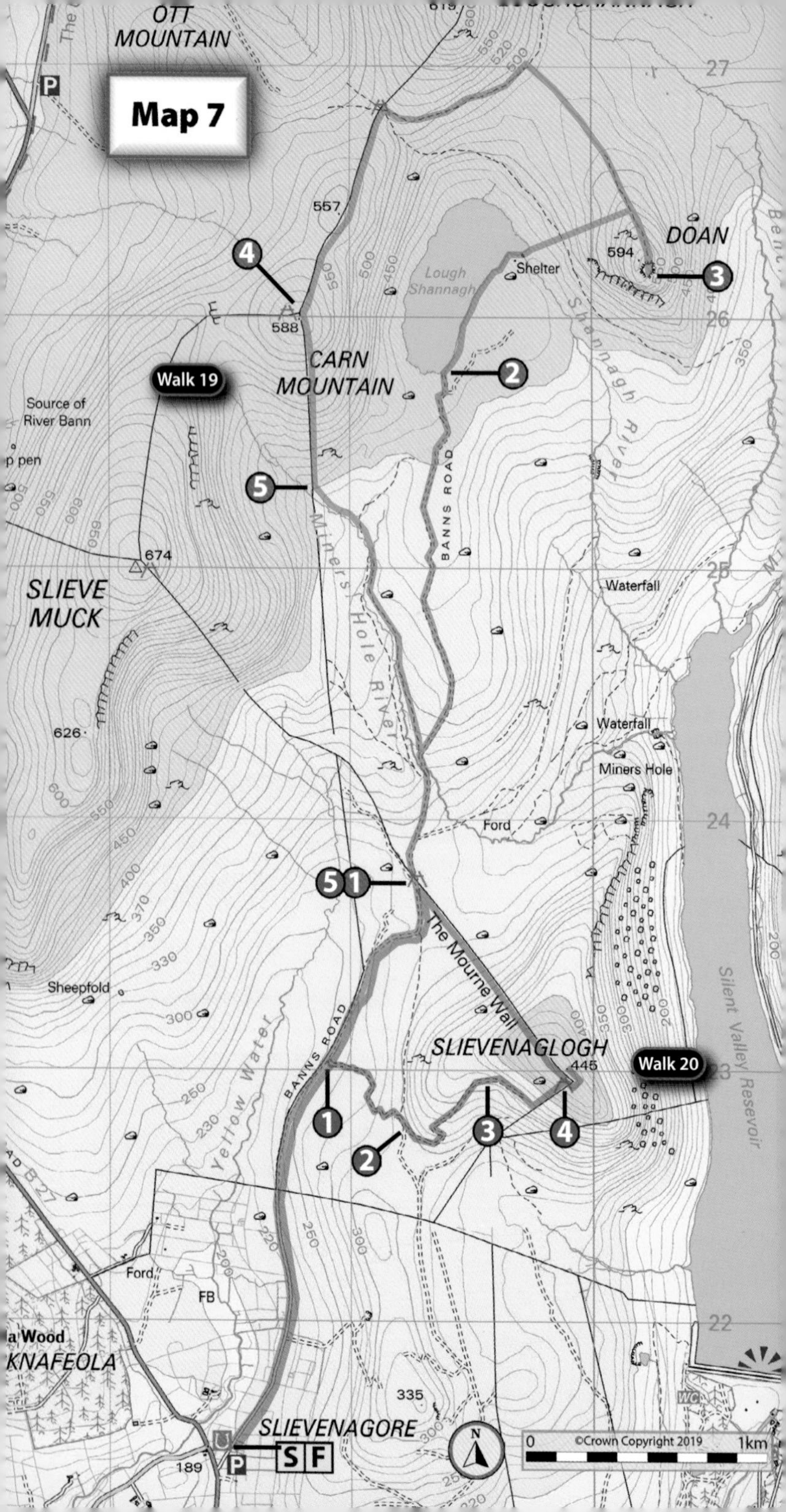
Map 7
OTT MOUNTAIN
DOAN
Lough Shannagh
Shelter
Shannagh River
CARN MOUNTAIN
Walk 19
Source of River Bann
BANNS ROAD
Miners' Hole River
SLIEVE MUCK
Waterfall
Miners Hole
Ford
The Mourne Wall
Sheepfold
Yellow Water
SLIEVENAGLOGH
Walk 20
Silent Valley Reservoir
FB
KNAFEOLA
SLIEVENAGORE
S F
©Crown Copyright 2019
0
1km

19

Slieves Meelmore, Meelbeg and Bearnagh seen from the summit of Doan

S From the car park, head NE on a wide track bordered by dry-stone walls. After 15-20min, cross a stile and continue on the track (N) which passes along a stunning valley. Ahead on the left is Slieve Muck and in front, the triangular peak of Doan shows itself.

1 Cross a stile over the MW and continue N on a track. To the right, you will see the Ben Crom dam. After 5min, cross a bridge and continue SH. The track now becomes rocky and uneven: you may find a path, just to the right of the track, which heads in the same direction but is easier underfoot.

2 1:20: Arrive at the sparkling azure **Lough Shannagh (408m)** which is a popular picnic spot. TL off the main path to reach the shore of the lough. From there, TR and follow a small path which heads along the E side of the lough. Pass a stone shelter at the NE tip of the lough. Shortly afterwards, TR at a weir and proceed alongside a stream which narrows after a few minutes. Cross the stream on stones as soon as it is safe to do so. After crossing, TL and head back to the weir. Then TR and continue on the grassy path along the edge of the lough. When the path disappears, continue SH (ENE) straight up the hillside towards a ridge: the terrain is wet and boggy but you may find a faint path in places. On the ridge, TR and climb on a clear path. When the path splits, in front of a false summit which is just a rocky outcrop, take either path.

3 2:10: Arrive on the summit of **Doan (594m)** which offers superlative 360° views of the entire Mourne range. The seven highest peaks are clearly visible. Descend from the summit by retracing your steps. When you reach the point where you arrived on the ridge earlier, continue SH (NW) across a sandy plateau. Then, continue NW on a path which winds through peat hags but is not too difficult. If you lose the path, then just keep heading NW. On arrival at another clearer path, TL and head SW. When the path arrives at the MW, TL and walk uphill alongside it. After a while the path dips and then climbs again.

4 3:20: Arrive at the summit of **Carn Mountain (588m)**. Here the MW bends to the right (W) but you should follow another wall which stretches out ahead of you to the S.

5 3:35: The wall arrives at the Miners Hole River. Just before the river, the gradient steepens sharply: do not follow the wall down this steep gradient to the river. Instead, TL just before the gradient steepens and head SE to meet the river a few hundred metres further downstream. You may find a faint path. Watch your footing in the long grass. When you arrive at the river, continue walking downstream. After a few minutes, pick up a faint and narrow grassy path which continues downstream. Eventually, when the path meets the rocky track travelled earlier, TR and retrace your steps to the start.

20

The MW heading steeply up to the summit of Slieve Muck

S From the car park, head NE on a wide track bordered by dry-stone walls. After 15-20min, cross a stile and continue N on the track which now passes along a stunning valley. Ahead on the left is Slieve Muck and, in front, the triangular peak of Doan shows itself.

1 After another 5-10min, leave the track in favour of a faint grassy path on the right. This junction is easy to miss: if you reach a dry-stone wall (which meets the track from the N) then you have gone too far. For a while there is a stream running along the path. After about 5min, the path becomes grassy and heads S. Soon, it bends around to the left to work its way up the slopes to the E. After a few more minutes, ignore a faint path on the left and continue on the main path.

2 Just afterwards, at a junction, keep right (S). Immediately afterwards, at another junction, keep left and start to climb more steeply. Soon the Silent Valley Reservoir can be seen on the right.

3 When the path bends to the right to head directly towards the MW, ignore another path on the left. Shortly before the MW, pass through some stone ruins. Then, the path narrows to a small trail. TL at the MW and climb steeply alongside it.

4 1:15: After 5-10min, cross a stile over the MW. Immediately afterwards, follow the MW as it turns sharply left and then briefly follow a faint path NW to the summit cairn of **Slievenaglogh (445m)**. Retrace your steps back to the stile, cross over and follow the MW to the NW: there is a faint path near the wall through the heather. After a level section, descend steeply over rocks. When the route levels again the ground is boggy.

5 Arrive at a track known as Banns Road: TL and follow it back to the car park.

Slievenaglogh

20

Both the Silent Valley and Ben Crom reservoirs are visible from the summit

Due to its isolated position at the S side of the range, Slievenaglogh is not a well-trodden mountain. However, to overlook it is to miss out on grandstand views of the Slieve Binnian ridge and the Silent Valley. This short route provides an easier ascent of the mountain than that undertaken on the Mourne Wall Epic (Walk 29).

Paths are faint in places so care should be taken with navigation. The final part of the ascent is steep, as is the descent. The section of the descent just before Banns Road is quite boggy.

Time	2:15
Distance	7.1km 4.4miles
Ascent/Descent	251m 824ft
Maximum Altitude	445m 1460ft
Grade	Medium
Map	Map No. 7 (blue route)

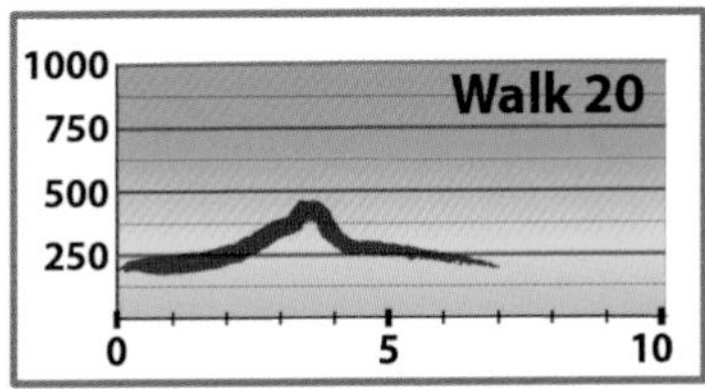

Start/Finish: Banns Road car park (194m; IG J 285214)

Access: From Newcastle, take the A50 NW towards Castlewellan. After just under 2 miles, TL onto the Ballyhafry Road (B180) towards Bryansford. Pass through Bryansford and then after 2¼ miles, TL at a junction ('Silent Valley'). Drive for 7.8 miles, passing Spelga Reservoir and Crocknafeola Forest, to arrive at a car park on the left beside a horse riding centre.

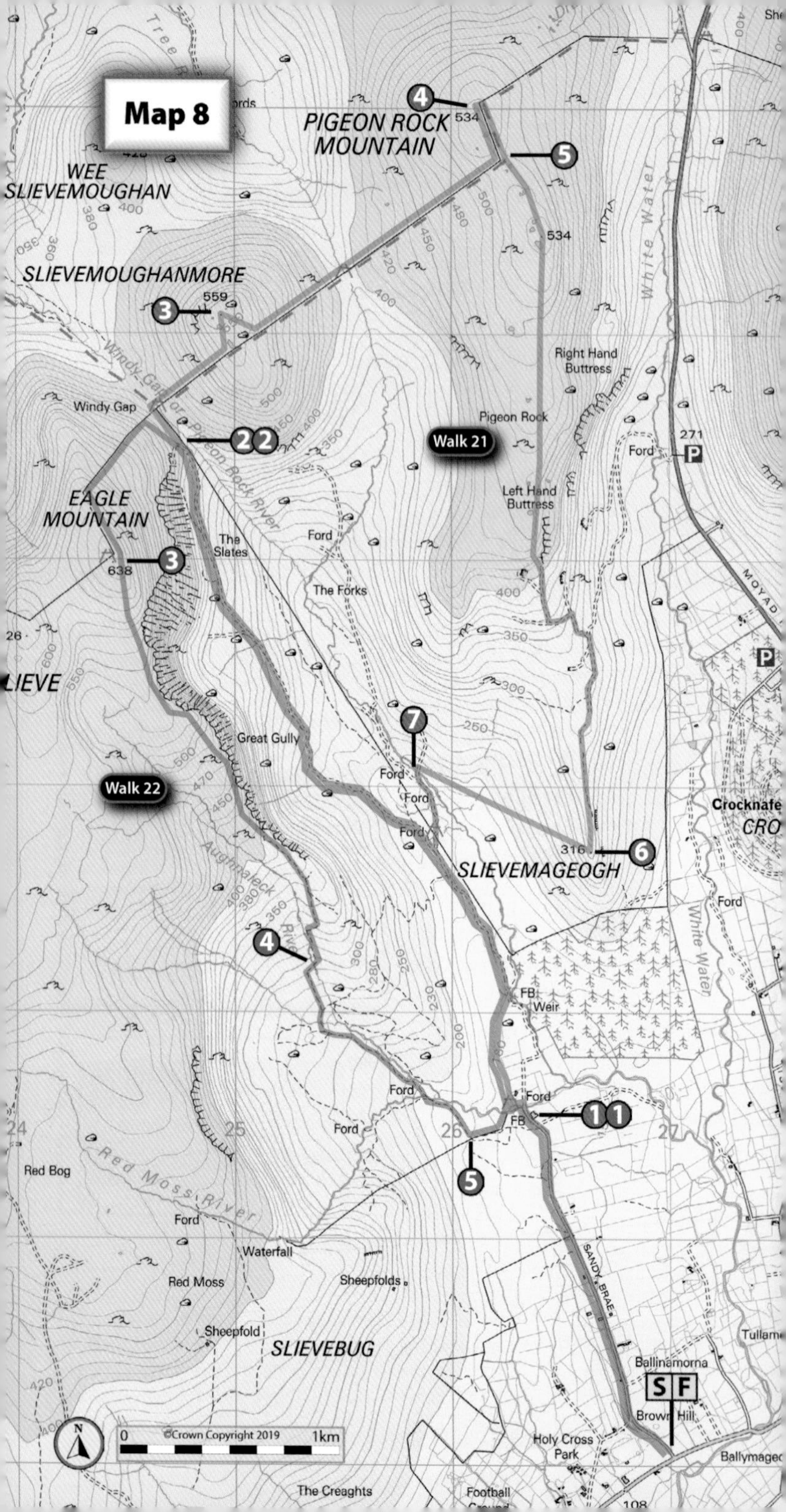

Map 8
PIGEON ROCK MOUNTAIN
WEE SLIEVEMOUGHAN
SLIEVEMOUGHANMORE
Windy Gap
Windy Gap or Pigeon Rock River
EAGLE MOUNTAIN
The Slates
The Forks
Ford
Right Hand Buttress
Pigeon Rock
Left Hand Buttress
White Water
Walk 21
Walk 22
Great Gully
Aughnaleck River
SLIEVEMAGEOGH
Crocknafe
FB
Weir
Red Bog
Red Moss River
Red Moss
Waterfall
Sheepfolds
Sheepfold
SLIEVEBUG
SANDY BRAE
Ballinamorna
Brown Hill
Holy Cross Park
The Creaghts
Football Ground
Ballymageo
Tullame
MOYAD
©Crown Copyright 2019
0
1km

The Pigeon Rock Ridge

21

A cold morning on the summit of Slievemoughanmore

This rewarding route takes you across some of the least-travelled ground in the whole range. After a long beautiful walk up through the Pigeon Rock River Valley, climb Slievemoughanmore and then Pigeon Rock Mountain. From there, keep your altitude for some time as you traverse the rugged and isolated Pigeon Rock Ridge which is dotted with pretty little tarns.

Whilst the altitude gain/loss is moderate, the route is quite long and some of the ground is wet and boggy in autumn and winter. There is no path on the Pigeon Rock Ridge so the route passes over grass and heather slopes and sometimes peat hags (which can be hard work).

Route finding is mostly straightforward as large sections of the walk are alongside dry-stone walls. However, navigation is tricky on the Pigeon Rock Ridge and it would be easy to lose your way in low visibility.

The route begins by heading N along Sandy Brae which was apparently used in season one of Game of Thrones as the entrance to Vaes Dothrak.

Time	5:00
Distance	16.0km 9.9miles
Ascent/Descent	710m 2330ft
Maximum Altitude	559m 1834ft
Grade	Hard
Map	Map No. 8 (red route)

Start/Finish: Attical (110m; IG J 270191)

Access: From the centre of Attical, follow the signs for 'Community Centre'. Drive about 1 mile SW on the Tullyframe Road to arrive at the Community Centre. Park on one of the verges along the Tullyframe Road or along Sandy Brae (the small road on the right immediately before the Community Centre). Park considerately as the roads are narrow and are used by farm vehicles. To shorten the walk, some people park at the N extremity of Sandy Brae where there is a large lay-by but it is not clear whether this is actually permitted.

S Head NW up a small road called 'Sandy Brae', which is just NE of the Community Centre and GAA sports club.

1 0:20: Pass a farm building on the right. Just afterwards, cross a river on a footbridge. TL immediately after the bridge to take a grassy path running W between the river and a dry-stone wall: do not go SH on the track as this is private property. Shortly afterwards, cross a stile and TR (N) to walk alongside a dry-stone wall. When the wall ends, keep SH alongside a sheep fence, still N: the path is very muddy here. Shortly afterwards, when the fence makes a 90° turn to the right, continue SH (N) aiming for a muddy track a short distance away. Pick up this track and follow it up the W side of the valley towards a saddle (known as the Windy Gap) which can be seen to the NW.

2 1:30: When the track arrives alongside a dry-stone wall, leave it and walk alongside the wall for a few minutes up to the **Windy Gap (407m)**. There are two stiles there: cross the left one, over another dry-stone wall. Then, TR and walk uphill with the wall on your right. After 15-20min of steep climbing, when the gradient eases, TL (N) and climb towards a cairn on top of a rock.

3 2:00: From the cairn, head for another large cairn a few metres away to the NE: this marks the summit of **Slievemoughanmore (559m)**. The summit offers a splendid view of all the key peaks in the western Mournes including Cock, Hen, Pigeon Rock and Eagle. It also provides one of the best views of Spelga Dam. Head SE and descend to arrive back at the wall again: descend alongside it. The route is steep and slippery in places. At a saddle, keep SH and climb NE still alongside the wall. Eventually, follow the wall as it bends around to the left.

4 2:30: After a few more minutes, arrive at the cairn and stile on the broad, flat summit of **Pigeon Rock Mountain (534m)**. Climb the stile over the wall and TR, heading back the way you came (S) with the wall on your right.

5 Leave the wall where it makes a 90° turn to the right and head SSE up a rock and heather slope. After a few minutes, head for a cairn which can be seen to the S. From there, continue S along the top of the broad ridge: there is no path and there are some energy sapping peat hags. The views, however, are spectacular: to the E is Slieve Muck and to the W, Slievemoughanmore and Eagle Mountain. Stay S along the crest of the ridge and do not head towards a small peak further to the W which seems to draw you towards it like a magnet. Eventually, arrive at a track on the ridge: follow it as it zigzags downwards to arrive at another track. TR and keep S along the ridge.

6 4:00: Arrive on the summit of **Slievemageogh (316m)** at the end of the ridge. From there, descend NW down the steep grassy slope towards a gate in a dry-stone wall far below.

7 Cross the Pigeon Rock River at a ford and pick up a faint track running to the gate. Cross the wall using a stile beside the gate. Then TL and walk up a track. Shortly afterwards, on arrival at the track travelled earlier, TL and retrace your steps to the start.

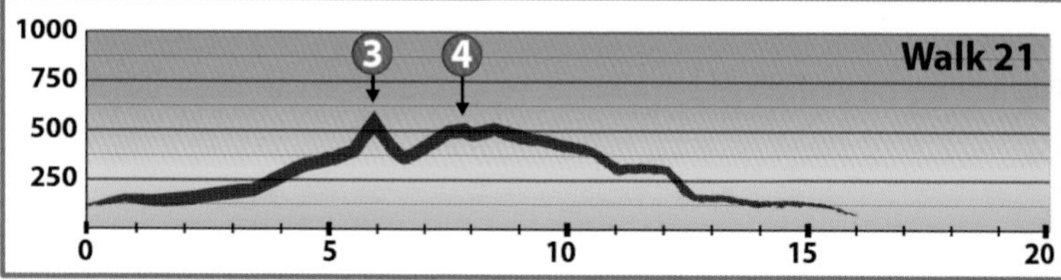

Eagle Mountain

Follow Batt's Wall to the summit

Eagle Mountain is one of the quietest peaks in the entire range which is surprising given that it offers one of the finest viewpoints. After a long beautiful walk up through the Pigeon Rock River Valley, climb to the summit. Then, enjoy a gentle descent as you make your way along a lovely ridge, right at the edge of some exhilarating cliffs.

Time	3:40
Distance	11.9km 7.4miles
Ascent/Descent	540m 1772ft
Maximum Altitude	638m 2093ft
Grade	Medium
Map	Map No. 8 (blue route)

The route mostly uses clear paths apart from the section between the summit and the cliffs. The sharp drops at the cliffs could be dangerous in low visibility when navigation would be tricky.

The route begins by heading N along Sandy Brae which was apparently used in season one of Game of Thrones as the entrance to Vaes Dothrak.

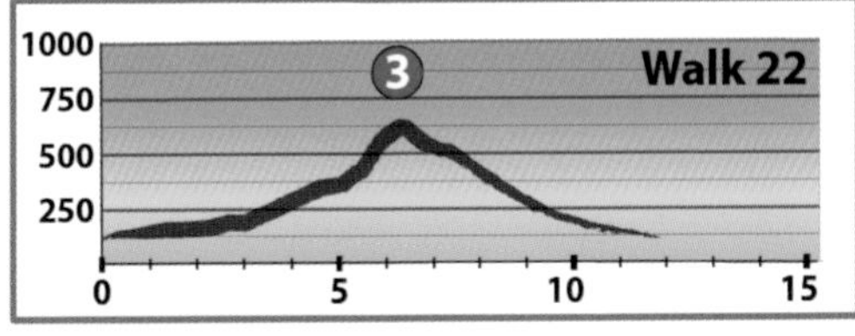

Start/Finish: Attical (110m; IG J 270191)

Access: From the centre of Attical, follow the signs for 'Community Centre'. Drive about 1 mile SW on the Tullyframe Road to arrive at the Community Centre. Park on one of the verges along the Tullyframe Road or along Sandy Brae (the small road on the right immediately before the Community Centre). Park considerately as the roads are narrow and are used by farm vehicles. To shorten the walk, some people park at the N extremity of Sandy Brae where there is a large lay-by but it is not clear whether this is actually permitted.

22

The rarely climbed Eagle Mountain has some of the finest views in the Mournes

S Head NW up a small road called 'Sandy Brae', which is just NE of the Community Centre and GAA sports club.

1 0:20: Pass a farm building on the right. Just afterwards, cross a river on a footbridge. TL immediately after the bridge and take a grassy path running W between the river and a dry-stone wall: do not go SH on the track as this is private property. Shortly afterwards, cross a stile and TR (N) to walk alongside a dry-stone wall. When the wall ends, keep SH alongside a sheep fence, still N: the path is very muddy here. Shortly afterwards, when the fence makes a 90° turn to the right, continue SH (N) aiming for a muddy track a short distance away. Pick up this track and follow it up the W side of the valley towards a saddle (known as the Windy Gap) which can be seen to the NW.

2 1:30: A few hundred metres from the Windy Gap, the path nears a dry-stone wall on the right. Do not drop right to walk alongside the wall: instead keep SH on the path climbing to the NW. Arrive at another wall which heads steeply up to the left: the Windy Gap is just down to the NE. TL and climb alongside the wall. Directly behind you is the flat top of Slievemoughanmore. Continue following the wall when it bends sharply to the left. Then, when it bends to the right, keep SH (SE) for a few metres.

3 2:00: Arrive at the summit cairn of **Eagle Mountain (638m)**. The views from this peaceful mountain are magnificent. Head S on a faint grassy path. When this disappears, continue S across heather towards flatter ground just to the right of some cliffs. Just before reaching the cliffs, pick up a path heading S. At the cliffs, TL at a junction of faint paths (SE) and walk along the edge of the cliffs. Watch your footing as the drops are severe in places. Keep following the path S when it finally withdraws from the edge of the cliffs a little.

4 Ford a stream on some boulders. Shortly afterwards, TL at a junction and continue S for a few minutes. Cross another stream and go SH, still S. Shortly afterwards, the path bends to the left and follows the stream gently downhill to the SE. Just ahead now are the buildings at the top of Sandy Brae. After a while, the path fords another stream. Immediately afterwards, TL and follow this stream downhill, still on the path. After a few more minutes, the path bends to the right away from the stream.

5 TL at a fence and walk downhill alongside it. Keep following the fence when it bends to the left. Then, cross the stream on some boulders. Cross the stile passed earlier, return to Sandy Brae and retrace your steps to the start.

Slieve Bearnagh & the Silent Valley

Lough Shannagh: Doan is the peak on the right

A challenging and exceptionally scenic circuit around the beautiful Ben Crom and Silent Valley reservoirs. It also involves an ascent of Slieve Bearnagh, one of the Big Six: Bearnagh is the fourth highest mountain in the range and its rocky summit is one of the most recognisable from afar. Given its central position amongst many of the other high peaks, there are superb views from the summit.

Navigation can be a little tricky and sometimes the paths can be faint. In some places, the terrain is challenging and the ground can be wet or rocky underfoot. However, there are also easy sections like the walk alongside the Silent Valley Reservoir. The ascent and descent of Slieve Bearnagh are very steep and the summit should be avoided in bad weather or low visibility.

Time	7:00
Distance	22.4km 13.9miles
Ascent/Descent	790m 2592ft
Maximum Altitude	739m 2425ft
Grade	Very hard
Map	Map No. 9 (red route)

Start/Finish: Silent Valley Mountain Park (135m; IG J 306211)

Access: From Newcastle, take the A50 NW towards Castlewellan. After just under 2 miles, TL onto the Ballyhafry Road (B180) towards Bryansford. Pass through Bryansford and then after 2¼ miles, TL at a junction ('Silent Valley'). Follow the signs for 'Silent Valley' to arrive at Silent Valley Mountain Park: there is a small charge to enter. Check the gate closing times to avoid getting locked in. If in doubt, park outside the gates on the verges.

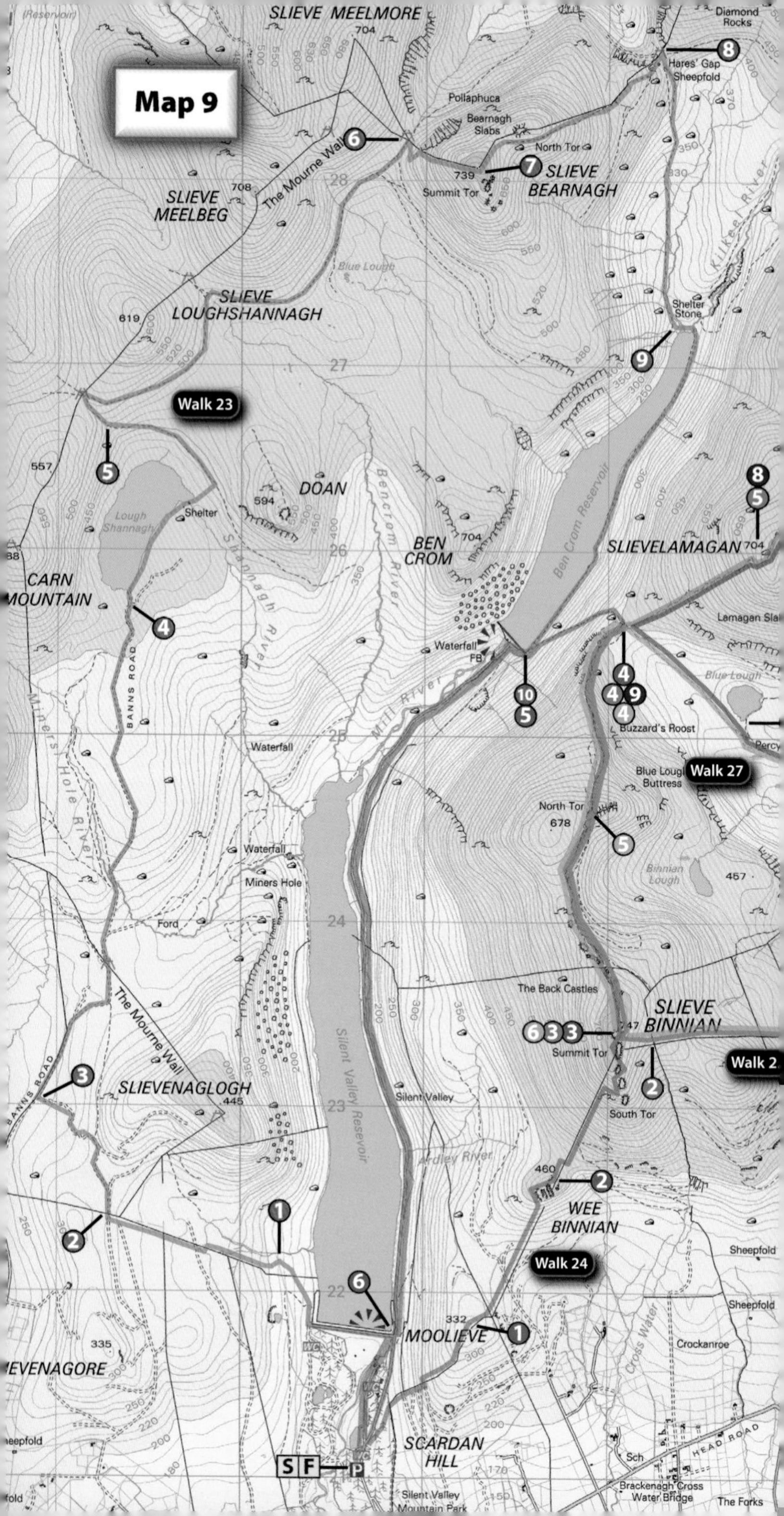

Map 9
Slieve Meelmore
Slieve Meelbeg
Slieve Loughshannagh
Slieve Bearnagh
Hares' Gap
Sheepfold
Diamond Rocks
Pollaphuca
Bearnagh Slabs
North Tor
Summit Tor
The Mourne Wall
Blue Lough
Shelter Stone
Kilkeel River
Walk 23
Lough Shannagh
Shelter
Doan
Ben Crom
Ben Crom Reservoir
Slievelamagan
Carn Mountain
Shannagh River
Bencrom River
Waterfall
Mill River
Banns Road
Miners' Hole River
Buzzard's Roost
Blue Lough Buttress
Walk 27
Percy
North Tor
Binnian Lough
Miners Hole
Ford
The Back Castles
Slieve Binnian
Summit Tor
South Tor
Slievenaglogh
Silent Valley Reservoir
Silent Valley
Ardley River
Wee Binnian
Walk 24
Sheepfold
Moolieve
Crockanroe
Cross Water
Scardan Hill
Silent Valley Mountain Park
Brackenagh Cross
Water Bridge
The Forks
Head Road
Sch

Climbing alongside the MW to the summit of Moolieve (Walk 24)

S From the car park, follow the road N past the Rangers' Office and a lake. At a junction, TL to walk up a tarmac lane. Shortly afterwards, at a fork, TR. At the Silent Valley Reservoir, TL and walk W along the top of the dam. At the SW corner of the reservoir, TR on a path along the edge of it. Soon, the path moves away from the water and starts to climb. A few metres afterwards, TR at a junction onto another path and continue climbing. Climb a stile and continue upwards.

1 The path makes a sharp left turn and then climbs to another stile. Do not cross it but TR to walk alongside a fence for a few metres until you reach the MW. Follow the MW upwards until the first stile over it: this section can be quite boggy. Cross the stile and keep following the MW to the W. Climb through a gap in another dry-stone wall which arrives from the left and continue uphill alongside the MW.

2 At the next stile, cross over and follow a broad grassy path N. After a few minutes, at a junction, keep left on the main path. After a few more minutes, at the next junction, TL onto a grassy path. Soon afterwards, TL at another junction.

3 Eventually, TR onto a wide track. After 5-10min, cross a stile over the MW and continue N on a track. To the right, notice the Ben Crom dam. After 5min, cross a bridge and continue SH. The track now becomes rocky and uneven. You may find a path, just to the right of the track, which heads in the same direction but is easier underfoot.

4 TL at a junction immediately before **Lough Shannagh** and proceed to the shore of the lough. Then, TR and follow a small path running close to the E shore. At times, the path winds its way through peat hags. Pass a stone shelter at the NE tip of the lough. Shortly afterwards, at a weir, TR and proceed alongside a stream which narrows after a few minutes. Cross the stream on stones as soon as it is safe to do so. After crossing, TL and head back to the weir. Then, TR and continue on the grassy path along the edge of the lough. At the head of the lough, head NE on a faint path running up the grassy slope slightly to the left. After a few minutes, the path bears left to contour around the hillside roughly parallel to the top of the lough. The path gradually continues bending to the left until you are heading W: it becomes faint and more grassy.

5 Just before a gully, the path bends right and climbs more steeply. Soon, enter the gully and climb the faint path up it. Just before the MW, turn sharp right onto another path. Soon, the path bears to the left and contours around the hillside. At times the path is faint.

6 Eventually, the path arrives at the saddle between Slieve Meelmore and Slieve Bearnagh: TR and climb, initially alongside the MW. Soon, the path drifts to the right up across the slope and then splits into a number of paths which appear to go in the same direction. Take the path furthest to the left (the steepest one) and climb. Then, work your way upwards, soon drifting back towards the MW again: arrive back at the MW just above the point where it re-emerges at the top of some steep crags. Now climb steeply alongside the MW, working your way up through rocks. Just before the summit, pick up a clear path.

7 4:00: Arrive at the summit plateau of **Slieve Bearnagh (739m)**. To get to the very top you would need to scramble the last few metres up the rocks on the summit: if you wish to do this then take care. From the summit, follow the wall downhill to the NE. After a few minutes, bear right around some boulders and then follow a path E around the base of the North Tor of Slieve Bearnagh. There are a number of paths: use the widest one, which is roughly in the middle. The path circles around the North Tor to arrive back at the MW again: follow it steeply downhill. Eventually, the path levels out and skirts to the right of

23

The MW running over the North Tor of Slieve Bearnagh

a group of rocks. Afterwards, the path continues to drift away from the MW. When it arrives at another path, TL and descend steeply on some rock steps.

8 TR at the large cairn on the **Hares' Gap (437m)**, heading S. Soon afterwards, pick up a faint path heading across the slope towards the valley below. Note that there are two paths here: choose the lower one. If you lose the faint path, then just head S towards the Ben Crom Reservoir.

9 At the **Ben Crom Reservoir**, cross the river flowing into it on some large boulders and pick up a path on the other side: take care as the rocks are slippery. Soon afterwards, ford another river and follow a path along the SE side of the reservoir: this path is rocky and undulating so it is hard going.

10 At the foot of the reservoir, climb a stile and descend on steps to a tarmac track. TL and walk along the track, at first beside a river and then the Silent Valley Reservoir. Look out for the Binnian tunnel on the left which carries water from the Annalong Valley to the Silent Valley: it was opened in 1952 and took 150 men to build. At the SW corner of the reservoir, leave the tarmac and descend some steps to pick up a path heading SW. Follow the red arrows to return to the car park (via the old water treatment works).

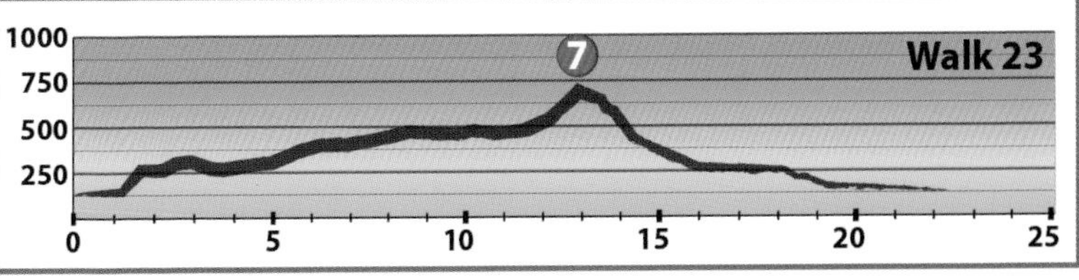

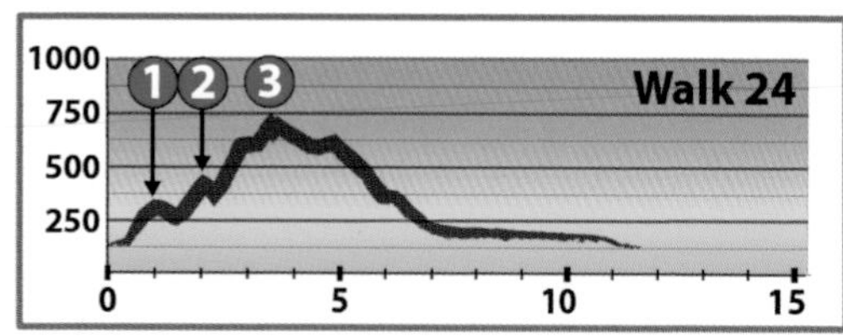

S From the car park, follow the road N past the Rangers' Office and a lake. At a junction, cross the road (E) and enter woodland to pick up a path. After a few metres, TL at a fork and head NE. After 5min, emerge from the forest and shortly afterwards, arrive at a junction: turn sharply right and head briefly along a grassy path to a stile over the MW. Cross over and climb uphill on a path alongside the MW. There are great views of the Silent Valley reservoir to the N. The path steepens as you progress. After 5-10min, cross the MW using another stile and continue uphill, still alongside it.

1 0:40: Arrive at the broad, flat summit of **Moolieve (332m)**. Descend briefly alongside the MW. Soon afterwards, at a junction of walls, descend NE to a saddle still with the MW on the right. From the saddle, climb again alongside the MW. Just before the MW terminates, upon arrival at the rocky outcrops of Wee Binnian, TL sharply away from the wall to skirt around the left of the outcrops. Towards the N of the outcrops, TR onto a small grassy path which continues upwards: some light scrambling may be required.

2 1:15: To the NE of the summit of **Wee Binnian (460m)**, pick up a path and descend (back alongside the MW again) to a stile. Cross the stile and climb alongside the MW (now on your left): the gradient gets progressively steeper and at times light scrambling may be required. When the MW terminates at some rocky outcrops, TR (SE) on a faint path. Shortly afterwards, TL and head N up a grassy slope. Soon, you will need to head NE to climb through a gap between the outcrops. Eventually, arrive at a little saddle flanked by interesting rock formations: TL (N) and climb on a path running across the base of a rock outcrop. On arrival at a grassy plateau, you can scramble a few more metres up the steep rocks onto the first summit tor of Slieve Binnian: take care as a fall here could have serious consequences and it is often very windy. To head for the main summit tor, from the grassy plateau, pass to the left of the first tor and descend some rocks to arrive at a path: TR and head up to the N.

3 2:30: Arrive at the main summit tor of **Slieve Binnian (747m)**. Be careful as it can be very windy on Slieve Binnian. Head N and walk along the crest of the ridge on a path heading towards a series of rocky outcrops. Head around to the left of the first set of outcrops and go through a gap in a dry-stone wall. Keep following the path and eventually, start to climb again. Pass to the left of the last rocky outcrop, the **North Tor (678m)**. Afterwards, the path descends: the Ben Crom Reservoir can be seen below. Shortly before a saddle, take care clambering down a short, but very steep, section of rocky steps.

4 3:20: At the saddle (398m), TL on a path heading initially NW. After a few minutes, ignore a path on the left. Soon, the main path bends to the SW, descending towards the Ben Crom Reservoir dam: there are a couple of alternative paths but they seem to interlink. Watch your footing on a few sections of large boulders.

5 At the dam, climb a stile and descend on steps to a tarmac track: TL and walk along the track, at first beside a river and then the Silent Valley Reservoir. Look out for the Binnian tunnel on the left which carries water from the Annalong Valley to the Silent Valley: it was opened in 1952 and took 150 men to build.

6 Arrive at a junction just S of the Silent Valley Reservoir dam. Leave the tarmac and descend some steps to pick up a path heading SW. Follow red arrows to return to the car park (via the old water treatment works).

Moolieve & the Binnians

24

The North Tor of Slieve Binnian and Binnian Lough

A fabulous walk over three peaks, two of which, Moolieve and Wee Binnian, are rarely climbed. The third peak is the wonderful Slieve Binnian which features in a few other walks in this book, however, this is a different and unconventional approach to it. The route also traverses the incredible Binnian ridge and descends to the scenic Ben Crom and Silent Valley reservoirs.

The climb all the way to the summit of Slieve Binnian is steep and tough but the MW provides guidance most of the way. Just before the summit, however, the MW terminates at a sheer rock face: good navigation skills are required to pick your way up through the rocky outcrops to the summit and this should not be attempted in bad weather or low visibility. The wind can be fierce around the summit of Slieve Binnian.

Time	4:45
Distance	11.7km 7.3miles
Ascent/Descent	870m 2854ft
Maximum Altitude	747m 2451ft
Grade	Hard
Map	Map No. 9 (blue route)

Start/Finish: Silent Valley Mountain Park (135m; IG J 306211)

Access: From Newcastle, take the A50 NW towards Castlewellan. After just under 2 miles, TL onto the Ballyhafry Road (B180) towards Bryansford. Pass through Bryansford and then after 2¼ miles, TL at a junction ('Silent Valley'). Follow the signs for 'Silent Valley' to arrive at Silent Valley Mountain Park: there is a small charge to enter. Check the gate closing times to avoid getting locked in. If in doubt, park outside the gates in the verges.

The heather covered slopes of the Annalong Valley with Slieve Donard in the background

The Annalong Valley Horseshoe

25

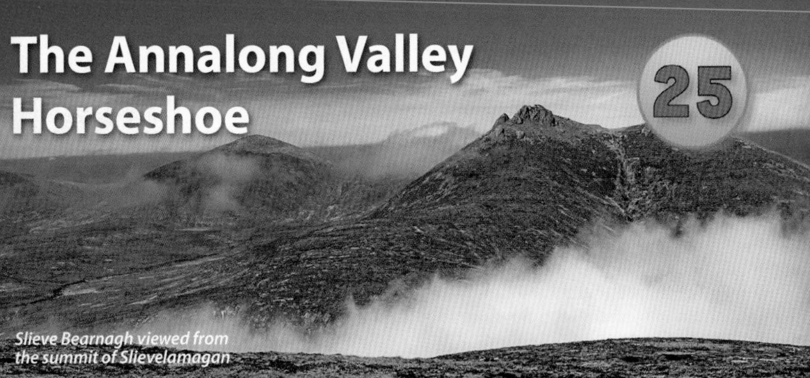
Slieve Bearnagh viewed from the summit of Slievelamagan

This epic route is one of the finest in the Mournes. The first half takes you along the crest of an amazing ridge running from S to N through the very heart of the range. The central position of the ridge means that everywhere you look there is stunning scenery to absorb and peaks to identify. Slieve Donard looms large throughout the day. Along the way, climb two of the Big Six (Slieve Binnian and Slievelamagan).

After descending from the main ridge, the route makes its way along the Brandy Pad, a popular old smugglers' route from which the views down the Annalong Valley are magnificent. Finally, there is a quick ascent of Rocky Mountain (which is rarely climbed due to its inaccessible location) to round off the day. It is a long but immensely rewarding outing.

Time	7:00
Distance	19.9km 12.4miles
Ascent/Descent	1220m 4003ft
Maximum Altitude	747m 2451ft
Grade	Very hard
Map	Map No. 9 (green route)

The ascents of both Slieve Binnian and Slievelamagan are steep but the latter is particularly tough: although there is a path indicated on the maps, we have trouble locating it. There is no getting away from the fact that Slievelamagan is a tricky climb and there is nothing for it but to take the direct route, from top to bottom, across the rocks and heather. Finally, bear in mind that navigation on the ridge is difficult in low visibility so save this route for a fine day. There are steep cliffs on the ridge: a fall could be serious.

Start/Finish: Carrick Little car park (160m; IG J 345219)

Access: From Newcastle town centre, follow the signs for 'Kilkeel A2'. Head SE out of Newcastle and, after a few miles, pass the Bloody Bridge car park on the left. About 4 miles after Bloody Bridge, TR ('Silent Valley') onto Quarter Road. After 2½ miles on this narrow and winding road, arrive at Carrick Little car park on the right.

S From the information board in the car park, head N on a track. After 15min, go through a gate and proceed SH on a path running parallel to the MW. Straight away, the views are fabulous. Many of the highest peaks are visible including Slieve Binnian, Slievelamagan, Slieve Commedagh and, tucked in behind Rocky Mountain (which you will climb on the return), Slieve Donard.

1 When the path forks, TL to follow a rocky path heading upwards to the NW, still parallel to the MW. Where the MW is bisected by another wall, keep SH and continue to follow the MW. About 1hr from the start, the rocky summit of Slieve Binnian comes into view ahead.

2 Arrive at a stile, a few hundred metres before the MW terminates at the base of some cliffs. Just afterwards, the path starts to head to the right away from the MW and climbs very steeply towards a cleft in the summit cliffs.

3 1:30: Pass through the cleft and TR to arrive at the summit of **Slieve Binnian (747m)**. The views are stunning. Head N and walk along the crest of the ridge on a path heading towards a series of rocky outcrops. Head around to the left of the first set of outcrops and go through a gap in a dry-stone wall. Keep following the path and eventually, start to climb again. Pass to the left of the last rocky outcrop, the **North Tor (678m)**. Afterwards, the path descends: the Ben Crom Reservoir can be seen below. Shortly before a saddle, take care clambering down a short, but steep, section of rocky steps.

4 2:40: At the **saddle (398m)**, continue SH on a path heading NE straight up the slopes of Slievelamagan. Soon the path disappears and unfortunately, there is no easy way up this mountain: you may find sheep tracks here or there but there is no alternative to having to work your way upwards (NE) over the peat and heather directly towards the summit. In places, this entails clambering over rocks.

5 3:20: From the summit of **Slievelamagan (704m)**, follow a path along the ridge (initially NE). After a few minutes, ignore a path on the right and keep on the wide rocky path which now descends just to the left of the crest of the ridge. Descend to a **saddle (553m)** and then continue up the slope on the other side. Soon afterwards, at an indistinct fork, you can go either left or right: the left fork goes directly to the summit of Cove Mountain but the right fork takes you on a thrilling path along the edge of the cliffs to the E of the ridge. The latter is recommended but watch your footing near the cliffs as a fall could have serious consequences. If you take the right fork, eventually the path comes to a dead end: TL and climb directly up the slope (there is no path).

6 From the summit cairn of **Cove Mountain (655m)**, head N to pick up a path and descend to another saddle: continue on a wide path heading uphill on the other side of the saddle.

7 Pass the **Devil's Coachroad**, an aptly named gully descending steeply through the cliffs to the valley below: watch your footing here. The summit of **Slieve Beg (596m)** is a few metres away to the NE. From the summit, head NE on a path which soon descends.

8 4:30: Arrive at a large cairn beside the **Brandy Pad**, an old smugglers' route: for further information see Walk 12. TR and walk along the Brandy Pad which contours around the hillside. At a fork, TR.

9 5:00: When the Brandy Pad arrives at the MW, TR and walk along the right side of it. This section can be wet and boggy so some people like to walk along the flat top of the MW instead. However, we cannot condone this as a fall from the MW could be serious.

10 After 25min, where the MW angles to the left, the path bends to the right away from the MW. After a few metres, TR on another path to head almost back the

The home straight, heading towards Rocky Mountain alongside the MW

25

way you have just come (NW). After a few minutes, the path becomes faint but keep following it until it bends around to the W. Then, TL and leave the path to head S up the grassy slopes directly towards the summit of Rocky Mountain: there is no path.

11 5:50: Arrive at the summit of **Rocky Mountain (525m)**. Note that there are two Mourne peaks known as 'Rocky Mountain': the other one is to the W of the range (see Walk 17). Continue S and descend. After a few minutes, pick up a faint path which descends SE towards a stile over the MW. If you cannot find this path then simply work your way down the slope towards the SE. Make sure that you do not stray too far towards the W as that part of the slope is very steep. TR at the stile and walk alongside the MW. After about a minute, when the path forks, TR and proceed along a rocky path: this junction is easy to miss.

12 Eventually, the path arrives at a dry-stone wall and follows the wall gently downhill (SW). When the path arrives at a stile, climb over and TL to proceed along a grassy track. After a few more minutes, go through an iron gate and continue on the track. At a road, TR and walk along it for 20min to return to the car park.

The Annalong Valley

S From the information board in the car park, head N on a track. After 15min, go through a gate and proceed SH on a path running parallel to the MW. From here, you can see many of the peaks of the high Mournes including Slieve Binnian, Slievelamagan, Slieve Commedagh and, tucked in behind Rocky Mountain, Slieve Donard.

1 When the path forks, TR following a fence NW. After 20min, pass a dry-stone wall. Shortly afterwards, TR heading NE on a path running up the Annalong Valley.

2 After 10min cross a stream. Shortly afterwards, TR onto another path: this junction is easy to miss (IG J 336250). After a while, the path becomes rocky and tricky underfoot. It climbs higher up the W slopes of the valley and then narrows to a trace. Ford a stream on some rocks. Then pick your way through boulders generally N. Eventually, the path gets closer to the river again and heads directly towards the cliffs of Slieve Beg: it is sometimes faint.

3 The path bends to the right (NE), fords a stream and climbs. Now it becomes hard to follow and at times disappears over rocks. It bends to the N and then back to the NE again, running in front of the cliffs.

4 Eventually, the path arrives at a stream bed where water runs over granite slabs: there, the faint path bends to the left and at first climbs alongside the stream. The unusual rock formations ahead of you are known as the Castles. After a few minutes, cross the stream on the slabs and climb steeply on a faint path.

5 After 5-10min, TL onto the **Brandy Pad**, a famous smuggling route. For more information, see Walk 12. After 5min, TL at a large sprawling cairn, heading SW up the slope on a rocky path.

6 3:10: After 5-10min, keep SH across the summit of **Slieve Beg (596m)**. Shortly afterwards, pass a precipitous gully known as the **Devil's Coachroad**: take care. The path bends right (W) and descends towards a stream bed. Cross the stream bed and climb a steep path to the left of a line of boulders. Eventually, the line of boulders enters a broad rock garden: follow the faint path through the rocks directly up the slope.

7 3:40: At the broad, flat summit of **Cove Mountain (655m)**, head WSW. Shortly, pick up a faint path which soon heads SW. Take care not to stray too close to the dangerous cliffs to the S: it is extremely disorientating here in low visibility. After 5min, ignore a path joining from the right and continue SH. Descend to a broad saddle and climb up the other side on a rocky path. If you lose the path, keep heading S straight up the slope. Finally, the path bends back to the SW.

8 4:10: At the summit of **Slievelamagan (704m)**, head SW on a faint path which soon disappears. Keep descending steeply SW, working your way in and out of rocks, towards a saddle above Ben Crom Reservoir. There is no easy way down this slope and it is slippery in the wet.

9 At the saddle, TL onto a path heading SE. Pass the beautiful **Blue Lough** and continue SE. After 10-15min, TR at a junction. On arrival at the path travelled earlier, retrace your steps to the start.

Slievelamagan & the Annalong Valley

26

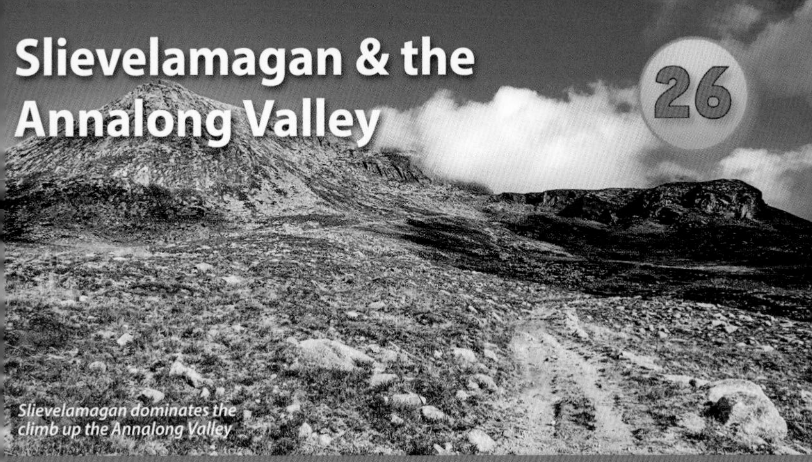
Slievelamagan dominates the climb up the Annalong Valley

This long route visits the peaceful heart of the Annalong Valley and travels the long central ridge of the high Mournes to the summit of Slievelamagan, probably the least accessible of the Big Six. The 360° views from the ridge and summit are beautiful.

Navigation at the N end of the Annalong Valley is tricky: the path is often faint or non-existent and the curves of the cliffs to the W make this a disorienting place, particularly in low visibility. It can also be tough going in the wet and there are some tricky rocky sections. The ridge is also a confusing place in low visibility and there are steep cliffs from which a fall could be fatal. Save this route for a clear day.

Time	5:30
Distance	16.0km 9.9miles
Ascent/Descent	840m 2756ft
Maximum Altitude	704m 2310ft
Grade	Hard
Map	Map No. 9 (purple route)

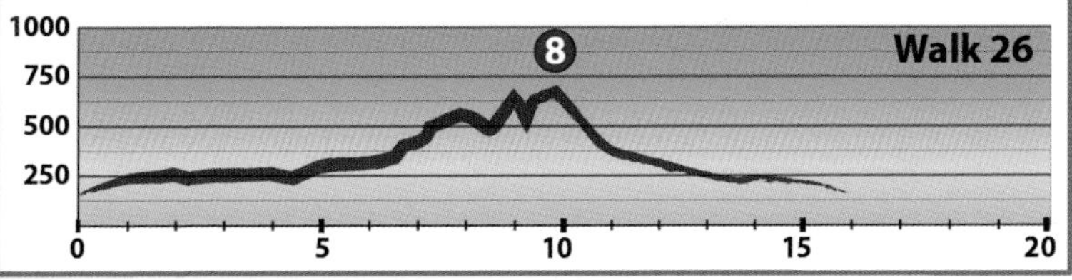

Start/Finish: Carrick Little car park (160m; IG J 345219)

Access: From Newcastle town centre, follow the signs for 'Kilkeel A2'. Head SE out of Newcastle and, after a few miles, pass the Bloody Bridge car park on the left. About 4 miles after Bloody Bridge, TR ('Silent Valley') onto Quarter Road. After 2½ miles on this narrow and winding road, arrive at Carrick Little car park on the right.

The descent back into the Annalong Valley

S From the information board in the car park, head N on a track. After 15min, go through a gate and proceed SH on a path running parallel to an incredible section of the MW.

1 0:20: When the path forks, TR following a fence NW. Straight ahead you can see Slievelamagan.

2 0:50: The path fords a broad stream. A few minutes later, TL at a fork just in front of a rock buttress.

3 1:10: Arrive alongside the lovely **Blue Lough (340m)**: a small path takes you the final few metres to the lough which, as its name suggests, is extremely blue. It is nestled beautifully between Slievelamagan and Slieve Binnian. After viewing the lough, return to the main path and follow it NW towards a saddle between Slieve Binnian and Slievelamagan.

4 1:30: TL (SW) at a junction of paths on the saddle (398m) and climb the slopes of Slieve Binnian on a rocky path: it is steep in places and you will need to clamber over a few rocks. Towards the top, the path becomes faint and it can be easy to lose it.

5 Head to the right of the large rocky outcrops of the **North Tor (678m)**. Then, follow the path along the crest of the ridge. Approaching the next set of rocky outcrops, the path forks: TR and climb directly towards the outcrops. Head around the left side of the first outcrop. A few minutes later, pass through a gap in a dry-stone wall. Immediately afterwards, TR on a path heading all the way around the right side of another rocky outcrop. Immediately after the outcrop, head back up onto the crest of the ridge: ignore the faint path running SW. Head S along the crest of the ridge and pass a few more interesting rock formations.

6 2:45: Climb through a grassy cleft to arrive at the first summit of **Slieve Binnian (747m)**. The views are incredible on a fine day. From the first summit, follow the path S down to a little saddle a few metres away: from here, you can scramble up the second summit if you wish but watch your footing as the drops are very steep. From the little saddle, TL through another cleft in the rocks and then follow a faint path downhill to a dry-stone wall just to the E. TL and follow the wall downhill until finally, you arrive at the path travelled earlier. TR and retrace your steps to the start.

Slieve Binnian & Blue Lough

27

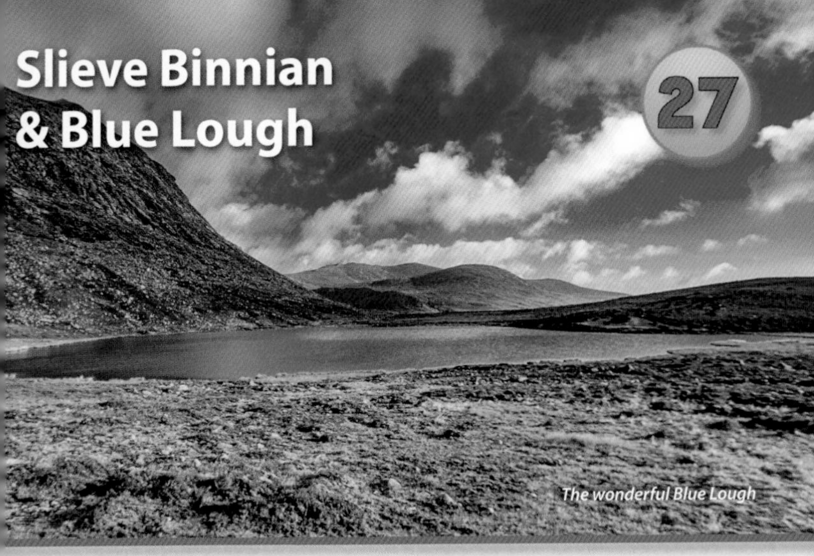

The wonderful Blue Lough

This half-day route summits one of the Big Six and travels the entire Slieve Binnian ridge, one of the finest traverses in the Mournes. The ridge is ideally positioned to offer superlative views of the Silent Valley and everywhere you look there is stunning scenery to absorb and peaks to identify. The ridge is also famous for its interesting rock formations.

The ascent of Slieve Binnian is steep and often muddy. There are also a few rocks to clamber over. Navigation is straightforward except on the steepest part of the climb where it is easy to lose the path. Avoid this walk in bad weather or low visibility.

Time	3:45
Distance	11.7km 7.3miles
Ascent/Descent	710m 2330ft
Maximum Altitude	747m 2451ft
Grade	Medium
Map	Map No. 9 (orange route)

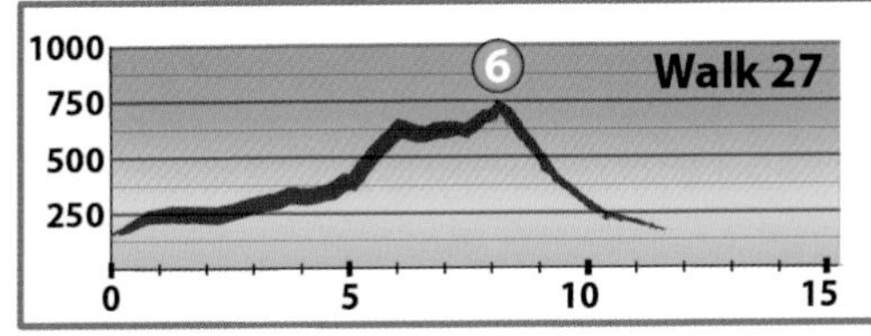

Start/Finish: Carrick Little car park (160m; IG J 345219)

Access: From Newcastle town centre, follow the signs for 'Kilkeel A2'. Head SE out of Newcastle and, after a few miles, pass the Bloody Bridge car park on the left. About 4 miles after Bloody Bridge, TR ('Silent Valley') onto Quarter Road. After 2½ miles on this narrow and winding road, arrive at Carrick Little car park on the right.

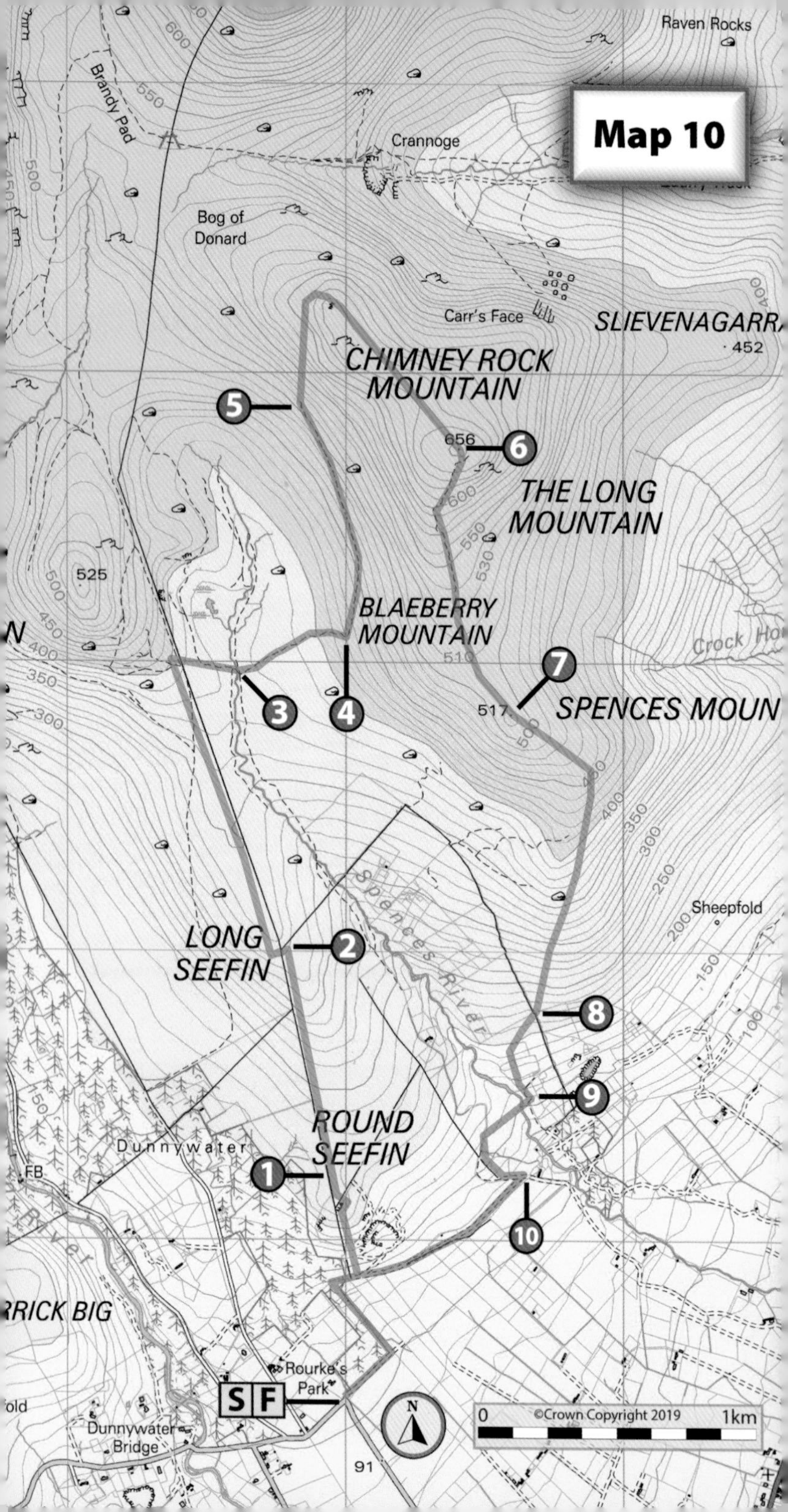
Map 10
Raven Rocks
Brandy Pad
Crannoge
Bog of Donard
Carr's Face
SLIEVENAGARR
452
CHIMNEY ROCK MOUNTAIN
656
THE LONG MOUNTAIN
525
BLAEBERRY MOUNTAIN
510
Crock Ho
517
SPENCES MOUN
Spences River
Sheepfold
LONG SEEFIN
ROUND SEEFIN
Dunnywater
FB
RRICK BIG
Rourke's Park
S F
Dunnywater Bridge
91
0
©Crown Copyright 2019
1km

Chimney Rock & the Seefins

28

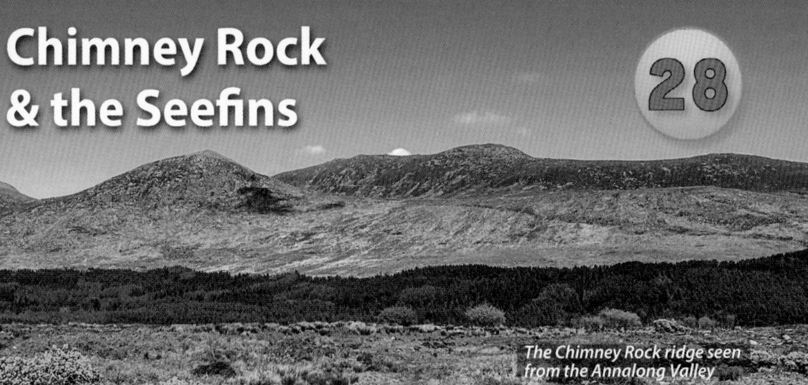
The Chimney Rock ridge seen from the Annalong Valley

This lovely circuit crosses some of the least-trodden parts of the Mourne Mountains. It is hard to understand why few people walk here because this is incredibly beautiful country. The route passes over a couple of minor peaks, Round Seefin and Long Seefin, before making a tricky ascent of the rarely climbed Chimney Rock Mountain. A tough but magnificent section follows, through heather and peat hags, along a broad ridge to Spences Mountain. The coastal views from here are exquisite and you are unlikely to encounter another soul.

Parts of the route are tough. The final ascent to Chimney Rock is steep and requires some light scrambling. Furthermore, the section from Chimney Rock to Spences Mountain, and the descent from Spences Mountain, are hard going as there are no paths and the ground is difficult underfoot. The lack of paths on some sections calls for navigation skills, particularly if visibility is limited. From experience, we can testify that the ridge between Chimney Rock and Spences Mountain is not a pleasant place to be during a storm.

Time	4:15
Distance	10.1km 6.3miles
Ascent/Descent	710m 2330ft
Maximum Altitude	656m 2152ft
Grade	Hard
Map	Map No. 10 (red route)

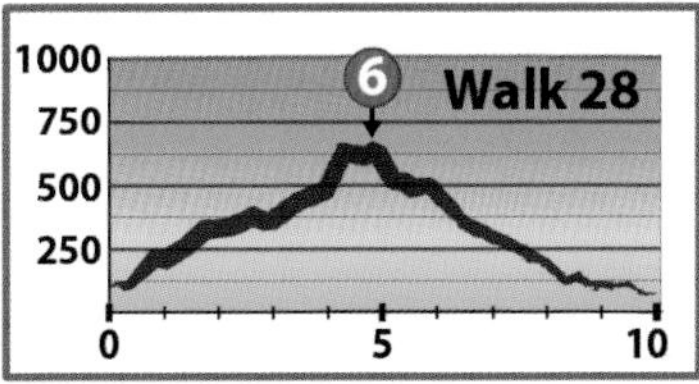

Start/Finish: Quarter Road near Annalong (105m; IG J 360224)

Access: From Newcastle town centre, follow the signs for 'Kilkeel A2'. Head SE out of Newcastle and, after a few miles, pass the Bloody Bridge car park on the left. About 4 miles after Bloody Bridge, TR ('Silent Valley') onto Quarter Road. After 1¼ miles, the road makes a 90° left hand bend. Park on the verge of the road, just before the bend: there is no formal car park.

S Head NE on a track which starts beside the bus stop, at the apex of the bend in Quarter Road. The broad track passes between trees and, after a few minutes, arrives at a gate. TL immediately before the gate onto a path ('Round Seefin footpath'). The path runs NE alongside a field, then bends to the right and arrives at a stile. Cross the stile and immediately afterwards, TL uphill on a faint path which climbs quite steeply close to a dry-stone wall on the left. After a few minutes, ignore a faint grassy path to the right. Behind you, the views across open farmland to the Irish Sea are fantastic. After 5-10min, the path veers to the right away from the wall, continuing to climb. Shortly afterwards, at a junction of paths, TL towards the wall again. The path now proceeds around the left side of a rocky outcrop. A few metres after the outcrop, cross a stile over a barbed wire fence. Immediately afterwards, TR and walk in front of another rocky outcrop ('Round Seefin'). After a few metres, the path turns sharply left and heads up through the rocky outcrop: this junction is easy to miss.

1 0:25: The path now heads back towards the wall and you are met with magnificent views of Slieve Binnian to the W. You are now on the summit of **Round Seefin (231m)**: follow the wall N. After 15-20mins, continue past a stone turret (which marks your arrival at the MW). Walk alongside the MW up onto the flat and barely discernible summit of **Long Seefin (350m)**.

2 A few minutes later, the MW meets another dry-stone wall. Just before this, cross the MW on stone steps. Continue climbing to the N on the other side of the wall. After 10min, cross a stile over the MW at the foot of Rocky Mountain. On the other side, pick up a faint rocky path heading E.

3 After a few minutes, ford Spences River and, on the other side, there is a choice of paths: ignore the paths running upstream and downstream alongside the river. Instead, head NE and, after a few metres, pick up a faint grassy path.

4 The path makes a sudden left turn and continues upwards to the N: it is now rocky but better defined. It climbs gently across the slopes with views of Slieve Commedagh and Slieve Donard to the N.

5 After 15-20min, the path bends to the right (N) and climbs more steeply. Shortly afterwards, before an old stone shelter (which is marked on the Harvey map), the grassy path terminates. This is where the hard work begins! Work your way steeply up the hillside through the rocks and heather generally to the N: there are no paths and some light scrambling may be required. After 15-20min of steep climbing, arrive on top of some rocky outcrops: pick up a path there and follow it SE. If you cannot find the path, simply head SE from the rocky outcrop.

The Mourne Wall near Long Seefin

6 2:30: Arrive at the summit cairn of **Chimney Rock Mountain (656m)**. On a fine day, this peak has some of the finest views in the Mournes. Descend S, making sure that you do not stray too far to the left as the slope gets steeper to the E. There is no path and the heathery ground is difficult underfoot. You should see the summit cairn of Spences Mountain ahead of you to the S.

7 3:00: From the summit of **Spences Mountain (515m)**, descend along the crest of the ridge, initially heading SE. Then, keep on the crest of the ridge as it bends around to the S. Again the heathery terrain is challenging so watch your footing. As you descend to the S, you will see a dry-stone wall ahead: make for a pair of farm gates in the wall.

8 Go through the left-hand gate and head across a field (SW) towards a gap in another dry-stone wall. From the gap, pick up a faint grassy track and follow it downhill through more dry-stone walls. After a few minutes, the track runs between a dry-stone wall and a sheep fence, alongside Spences River.

9 After a few more minutes, go through a gate on the right and pick up a grassy path heading downhill to the right. The path soon fords Spences River and continues on the other side. Soon, the path becomes faint as it winds its way SW through gorse towards another dry-stone wall. Just before the wall, TL onto a grassy track and descend. After a few minutes, pass a small red gate on your right.

10 Just before a house, arrive at a pair of farm gates on the right. Go through them and follow a path heading SW. Eventually, this path brings you back to the stile climbed earlier: cross it and retrace your steps to the start.

Map 11
Treatment Works
Fish Pass
FB
Weir
Fofanny Dam (Reservoir)
SLIEVENAMAN ROAD
SLIEVE MEELMORE
704
Pollaphuca
Bearnagh Slabs
North Tor
739
Summit Tor
SLIEVE BEARNAGH
708
The Mourne Wall
SLIEVE MEELBEG
Blue Lough
The Ulster Way
SLIEVE LOUGHSHANNAGH
619
OTT MOUNTAIN
557
Lough Shannagh
Shelter
594
DOAN
Bencrom River
704
BEN CROM
Ben Crom Reservoir
588
CARN MOUNTAIN
Shannagh River
BANNS ROAD
Waterfall
FB
Mill River
Miners' Hole River
674
Waterfall
North Tor
678
626
Waterfall
Miners Hole
Ford
The Back Castles
Summit Tor
Sheepfold
The Mourne Wall
SLIEVENAGLOGH
445
Silent Valley Reservoir
Silent Valley
Yellow Water
BANNS ROAD
Ardley River
460
WEE BINNIAN
Ford
FB
332
MOLIEVE
©Crown Copyright 2019
0
1km
SLIEVENAGORE
189

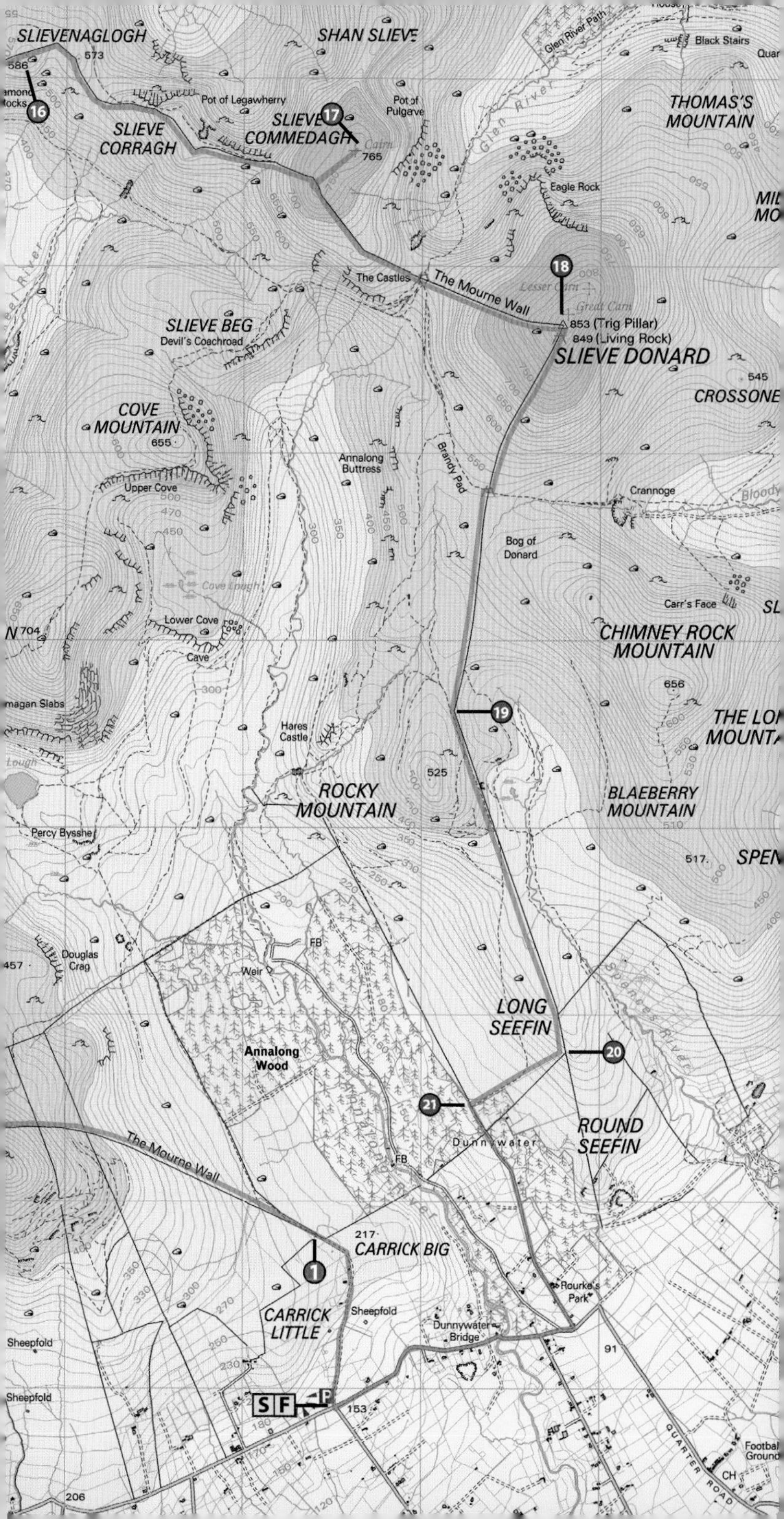

SLIEVENAGLOGH
586
573
SHAN SLIEVE
Glen River Path
Black Stairs
16
Pot of Legawherry
Pot of Pulgarve
SLIEVE CORRAGH
SLIEVE COMMEDAGH
17
Cairn
765
Glen River
THOMAS'S MOUNTAIN
Eagle Rock
18
The Castles
The Mourne Wall
Lesser Cairn
Great Cairn
853 (Trig Pillar)
849 (Living Rock)
SLIEVE DONARD
SLIEVE BEG
Devil's Coachroad
545
CROSSONE
COVE MOUNTAIN
655
Annalong Buttress
Brandy Pad
Upper Cove
Crannoge
Bog of Donard
Cove Lough
Carr's Face
Lower Cove
Cave
704
CHIMNEY ROCK MOUNTAIN
656
19
Hares Castle
THE LO MOUNTA
525
ROCKY MOUNTAIN
BLAEBERRY MOUNTAIN
Percy Bysshe
517
Douglas Crag
457
FB
Weir
LONG SEEFIN
20
Annalong Wood
21
Spences River
The Mourne Wall
ROUND SEEFIN
Dunnywater
FB
Annalong River
217
CARRICK BIG
1
Rourke's Park
CARRICK LITTLE
Sheepfold
Sheepfold
Dunnywater Bridge
91
Sheepfold
S F
P
153
QUARTER ROAD
Football Ground
CH
206

29
The Mourne Wall Epic is one of the longest ridge walks on the Island of Ireland
Walk 29
3
7
9
12
14
17
18
1000
750
500
250
0
5
10
15
20
25
30
35

The Mourne Wall Epic

29

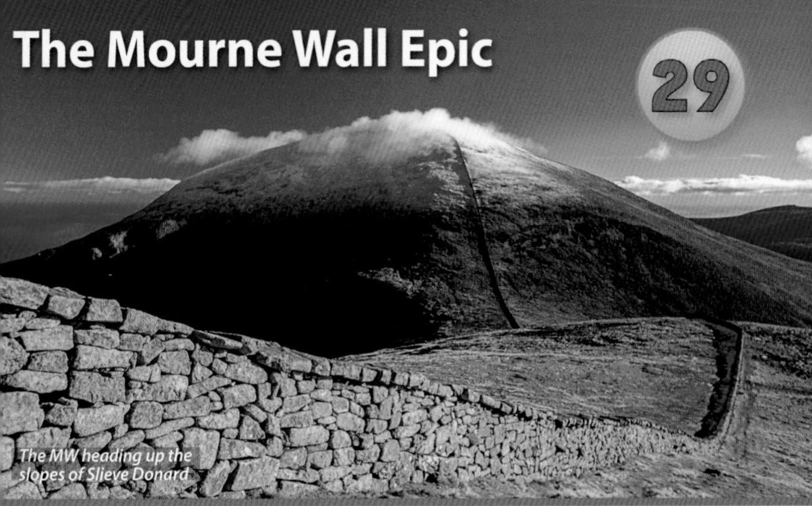

The MW heading up the slopes of Slieve Donard

This is the giant of them all and is arguably the longest and finest ridge walk in all of Ireland. It is also one of the hardest. The route involves almost a complete circumnavigation of the magnificent MW, climbing 15 named peaks on the way, including six of the seven highest mountains in the range. From the summit of Slieve Muck, you remain on the main Mourne ridge for an unbelievable 17km and the views are exquisite.

However, the terrain is relentless, alternately climbing and descending throughout. The very fit can complete the walk in one long summer day but it is more enjoyable to take two days, bivouacking somewhere along the way. An overnight beside the MW is a wonderful experience.

As the route has long, exposed sections, it is best saved for a fine day. Navigation is normally straightforward as mostly you follow the MW. However, finding safe passage between Slieve Binnian and Wee Binnian can be difficult. In this area, there are many cliffs and steep crags, which must be avoided.

Time	12-13 hours
Distance	33.4km 20.8miles
Ascent/Descent	2970m 9745ft
Maximum Altitude	849m 2786ft
Grade	Very hard
Map	Map No. 11 (red route)

Start/Finish: Carrick Little car park (160m; IG J 345219)

Access: From Newcastle town centre, follow the signs for 'Kilkeel A2'. Head SE out of Newcastle and, after a few miles, pass the Bloody Bridge car park on the left. About 4 miles after Bloody Bridge, TR ('Silent Valley') onto Quarter Road. After 2½ miles on this narrow and winding road, arrive at Carrick Little car park on the right.

The ground underfoot is a mixed bag: some sections use good paths but others are wet and boggy. There are also steep sections where a fall could have serious consequences. Summer is the best time for this challenging route because the ground is drier and the days are longer.

Some start the walk from the Silent Valley Mountain Park but we prefer to start from Carrick Little for two key reasons. Firstly, this enables you to tackle the hardest sections (between Slieve Binnian and Slieve Muck) early on, when you are freshest. Secondly, drinking water is a concern on this long route because there are few watercourses. A start from Carrick Little means that you can replenish your water supply closer to the half-way point: we find that the fast-moving Miners Hole River, near Waypoint 8, is the best source of water. There are livestock in the area so you should treat the water (by filtering, boiling and/or treating with chemicals) before drinking it. The various methods of treatment/purification differ in their effectiveness and are beyond the scope of this book so do your research before you set out. You drink the water at your own risk!

Note that confusingly there are two different peaks named Slievenaglogh which are climbed on this route.

S From the information board in the car park, head N on a track. After 15min, go through a gate and proceed SH on a path running parallel to the MW.

1 0:20: When the path forks, TL and follow a rocky path heading upwards to the NW, parallel to the MW. Where the MW is bisected by another wall, keep SH and continue to follow the MW.

2 Arrive at a stile, a few hundred metres before the MW terminates at the base of some cliffs. Just afterwards, the path heads to the right, away from the MW, and climbs very steeply towards a cleft in the summit cliffs.

3 1:30: Pass through the cleft and TR to arrive at the summit of **Slieve Binnian (747m)**. Retrace your steps from the summit back to the cleft. Head downhill to the W on a faint path towards the Silent Valley Reservoir. After a few metres, ignore another faint path on the left, which heads (underneath some crags) towards a section of the MW. Instead, continue downhill towards the reservoir. After a minute or so, leave the path and head SW down the grassy slope for a few metres until you pick up another faint path. TL and head towards the base of some boulders to the S. The path passes below some small sections of the MW and afterwards, becomes faint. Clamber down some large boulders: you will now be heading towards Wee Binnian, the rocky peak below to the SW. After a few more minutes, the MW comes into view again and the path brings you towards it. A few metres from the MW, the path descends steeply over shale, roughly parallel to the wall. Climb over the MW where it re-emerges at a rock slab. Take care here: there are some metal rods, driven into the slab on the other side of the wall, which may help you to scramble down carefully. Now simply follow the wall steeply downhill. At a saddle, cross the MW on a stile. Then climb, still alongside the MW.

4 2:00: When the MW disappears into some rock slabs, climb the last few metres to the summit of **Wee Binnian (460m)**. Head S for a few metres, then SW down through a steep cleft in the rocks. At a small grassy plateau, TR and head

N alongside the rocks of the summit, which is just above on the right. Pass through a narrow gap in the rocks and then descend NW for a few metres to pick up a path. TL and follow it, initially SW. The path bends to the left until it heads directly towards the MW again. When you reach the MW, follow it downhill. Cross a saddle and then climb. When the MW bisects another dry-stone wall, pass through a gap in the other wall and continue following the MW, initially W.

5 2:30: Arrive at the large boulder marking the summit of **Moolieve (332m)**. Continue following the MW, now to the SW. At a stile, cross the MW and continue descending alongside it. At the bottom of the slope, climb another stile: then TR and continue along a path. Shortly afterwards, keep SH at a junction, taking the right fork. After a few minutes, TR and walk along a tarmac lane to the SE tip of the Silent Valley Reservoir. TL and walk along the top of the dam at the foot of the reservoir. At the SW corner of the reservoir, TR on a path along the edge of the water. Soon, the path moves away from the reservoir and starts to climb. A few metres afterwards, TR at a junction onto another path and continue climbing. Climb a stile and continue upwards on the path. The path makes a sharp left turn and then climbs to another stile: do not cross it but TR to walk alongside a fence for a few metres until you reach the MW again. Follow the MW upwards: this section can be boggy.

6 When the MW makes a sharp turn to the right, keep following it. Pass through a gap in another dry-stone wall and continue steeply uphill alongside the MW. The path here is faint and intermittent and this is a tough little climb: at times you will need to clamber over rocks.

7 3:45: Pass a stile and immediately afterwards, when the MW turns sharply left, TL and follow a faint path to the summit cairn of **Slievenaglogh (445m)**. Retrace your steps back to the stile, cross over and follow the MW to the NW. There is a faint path near the wall through the heather. After a level section, descend steeply over rocks. When the route levels again the ground is boggy.

8 Keep SH across a track known as 'Banns Road', following the MW. The path becomes rocky and then bends left, away from the MW. After a while, pass through a gap in another dry-stone wall. Immediately afterwards, when the path disappears, TR and head to a stile in the MW. TL and climb with the MW on the right. When the MW disappears into rock slabs, skirt around them, well to their left, climbing steeply. You should aim to arrive back at the MW just where the wall re-emerges at the top of the slabs. Then, continue climbing very steeply next to the MW. When the wall disappears for a second time into some crags, climb up a small steep gulley which starts about 30m to the left of the MW. Pick up the MW again and continue climbing.

9 5:15: From the trig point on the summit of **Slieve Muck (674m)**, head towards two nearby stiles. Climb over the MW on the right hand stile. Then, TL and follow the MW to the N. After 20-25min, just before the MW bends sharply to the right, follow the path to the right, away from the wall, to skirt around a crag. Then continue alongside the MW again, now climbing.

10 5:45: Arrive at the summit cairn on **Carn Mountain (588m)**. Pass through a gap in another dry-stone wall. Then follow the MW when it bends to the left and heads to the N. The wall undulates for a while and then climbs quite steeply.

11 6:15: From the summit of **Slieve Loughshannagh (619m)**, descend to a saddle and then climb steeply again, still following the MW.

12 6:45: From the summit of **Slieve Meelbeg (708m)**, descend to another saddle and then climb up the other side. When the MW bisects another dry-stone wall, keep heading uphill (NE).

13 7:15: Cross a stile at a stone turret built into a corner of the MW. TL to reach the summit cairn of **Slieve Meelmore (687m)**. Cross back over the stile beside the turret and follow the wall SE downhill. Towards the bottom of the slope, the rocks are steep. At a saddle, start climbing, initially alongside the MW. Soon, the path drifts right up across the slope and then splits into a number of paths. Take the path furthest to the left (the steepest one) and climb. Now there is a confusing array of different paths: work your way upwards, soon heading back towards the MW again. Arrive back at the MW, just above the point at which it re-emerges at the top of some steep crags. Now climb alongside the MW, working your way up through rocks. Just before the summit, pick up a clear path.

14 8:00: Arrive at the summit plateau of **Slieve Bearnagh (739m)**. To get to the very top you would need to scramble the last few metres up the rocks on the summit. If you wish to do this then take care. From the summit, follow the MW downhill to the NE. After a few minutes, bear right around some boulders and then follow a path E around the base of the North Tor of Slieve Bearnagh. There are a number of paths here: use the widest one, which is roughly in the middle. The path circles around the North Tor to arrive back at the MW again. Follow the MW steeply downhill. Eventually, the path levels out and skirts to the right of a group of rocks. Afterwards, the path continues to drift away from the MW. When you reach another path, TL and descend steeply on some rock steps.

15 Keep SH (NE) past the large cairn at the **Hares' Gap (437m)**: climb steeply alongside the MW, to the right of a rocky outcrop.

16 9:00: From the summit cairn on **Slievenaglogh (586m)**, keep following the MW as it undulates along the ridge. Pass over the indistinct summit of **Slieve Corragh (641m)**. Descend briefly and then climb steeply. Cross a stile beside the turret near the summit of Slieve Commedagh and walk NE.

17 9:50: After a few minutes, arrive at the summit cairn of **Slieve Commedagh (765m)**. Retrace your steps back to the stile, climb over and descend SE alongside the MW. Cross a saddle and climb steeply.

18 10:45: Cross the stile at the summit of **Slieve Donard (849m)**, the highest point in Northern Ireland: TR and follow the MW downhill (SW), keeping on the E side of it. At the saddle at the **Bog of Donard**, cross a stile and continue S, now with the MW on your left. This section can be boggy so some people like to walk along the top of the MW instead. However, we cannot condone this as a fall from the MW could be serious.

19 Where the MW angles to the left, the path bends to the right away from the MW. After a few metres, TL at another path and walk SE. Eventually, arrive at the broad indistinct summit of **Long Seefin (350m)**: this is the last peak of the day although you would hardly notice it was there. Now descend.

20 When the MW makes a sharp turn to the right, at a lovely little turret, there are two walls running down to the SW. The most southerly one is the MW but the route is difficult where it heads into trees, so it is easier to follow the more northerly wall. From the turret, clamber down a few large rocks and then follow a path alongside the northerly wall.

21 Cross a stile beside an old iron gate: TL and walk along a track. After a few minutes, arrive back at the MW which continues to the right. On one side of the wall there is a forest which is too thick to walk through and on the other side there is private land so, unfortunately, this is the last you will see of the MW on this route. Go through a farm gate built into the MW and continue SH on a track. When the track arrives at a road, TR and walk along the road back to the car park.

Murlough National Nature Reserve

30

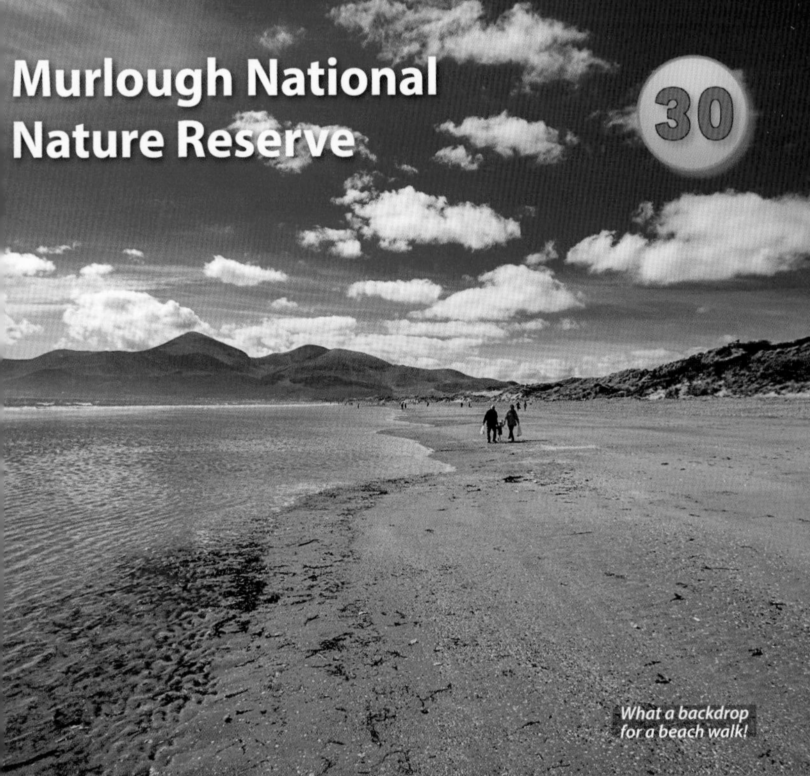

What a backdrop for a beach walk!

This is the only coastal walk in this book and it passes along a spectacular sandy beach with an incredible Mourne backdrop. It offers a completely different perspective of the Mourne range which is seen from further away. The beauty of the Murlough National Nature Reserve (**MNNR**) is such that, at times, it is very busy. But do not let that deter you as most visitors do not get further than the S section of the beach. Terrain and navigation are mostly straightforward. Altitude gain and loss are negligible so no elevation profile is provided here.

Time	1:45
Distance	6.0km 3.7miles
Ascent/Descent	40m 131ft
Maximum Altitude	19m 62ft
Grade	Easy
Map	Map No. 12 (blue route)

Start/Finish: Twelve Arches car park (345m; IG J 395342)

Access: From Newcastle, take the A2 north towards Dundrum. The car park is on the left after 2 miles.

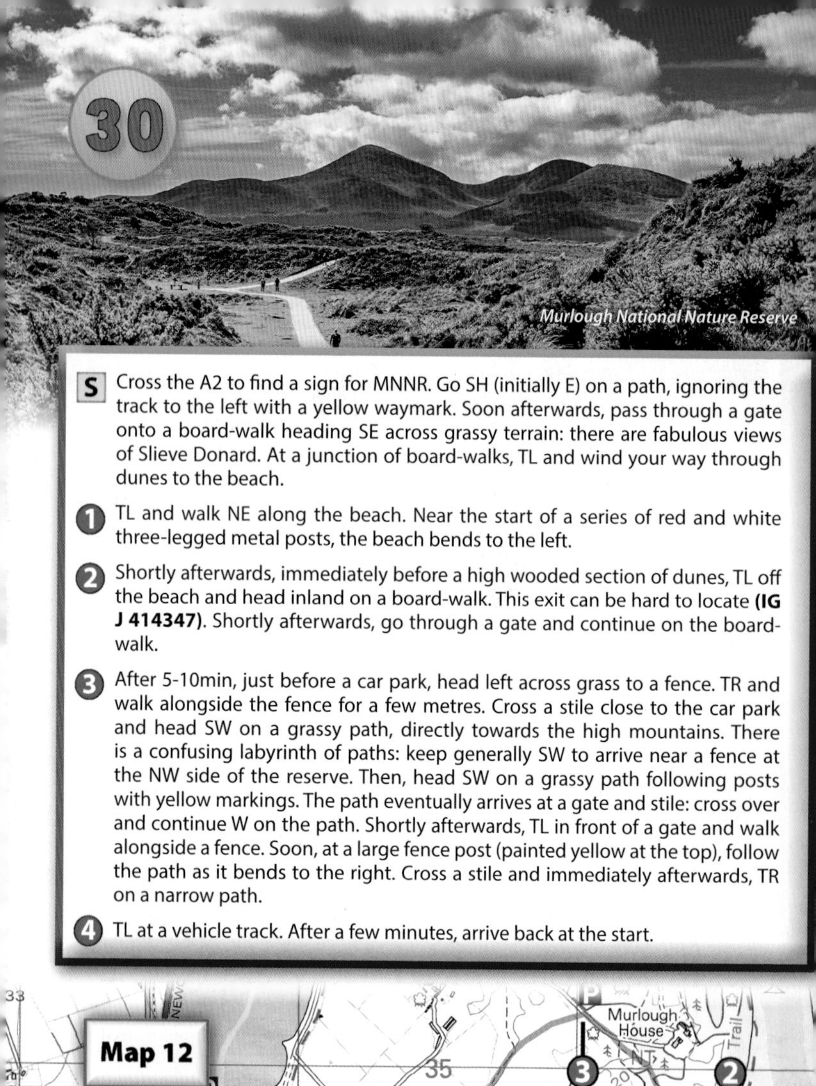

Murlough National Nature Reserve

S Cross the A2 to find a sign for MNNR. Go SH (initially E) on a path, ignoring the track to the left with a yellow waymark. Soon afterwards, pass through a gate onto a board-walk heading SE across grassy terrain: there are fabulous views of Slieve Donard. At a junction of board-walks, TL and wind your way through dunes to the beach.

1 TL and walk NE along the beach. Near the start of a series of red and white three-legged metal posts, the beach bends to the left.

2 Shortly afterwards, immediately before a high wooded section of dunes, TL off the beach and head inland on a board-walk. This exit can be hard to locate **(IG J 414347)**. Shortly afterwards, go through a gate and continue on the board-walk.

3 After 5-10min, just before a car park, head left across grass to a fence. TR and walk alongside the fence for a few metres. Cross a stile close to the car park and head SW on a grassy path, directly towards the high mountains. There is a confusing labyrinth of paths: keep generally SW to arrive near a fence at the NW side of the reserve. Then, head SW on a grassy path following posts with yellow markings. The path eventually arrives at a gate and stile: cross over and continue W on the path. Shortly afterwards, TL in front of a gate and walk alongside a fence. Soon, at a large fence post (painted yellow at the top), follow the path as it bends to the right. Cross a stile and immediately afterwards, TR on a narrow path.

4 TL at a vehicle track. After a few minutes, arrive back at the start.

Map 12

Murlough House
Newcastle Challenge Trail
Chambered Grave
Slidderyford Bridge
Murlough National Nature Reserve
Nursery
Dunes
Observe warning signs within this area
Safety Zone

©Crown Copyright 2019

0 — 1km

KILOMETRES

The view of Ben Crom Reservoir from the Binnian Ridge (Walks 24, 25 & 27)

Notes